A BEGINNERS' GUIDE
TO PRACTICAL ASTROLOGY

Other books by Vivian Robson:
The Fixed Stars and Constellations in Astrology
Electional Astrology
Astrology and Sex
A Student's Text-Book of Astrology
The Radix System
Alan Leo's Dictionary of Astrology (as editor)

A BEGINNERS' GUIDE

TO

PRACTICAL ASTROLOGY

BY

VIVIAN E. ROBSON, B.Sc.

Author of *A Student's Textbook of Astrology, The Fixed Stars and Constellations in Astrology,* etc.

BEL AIR
ASTROLOGY CLASSICS
1931

ISBN: 978 1 933303 36 9

This edition published 2010

Published by
Astrology Classics

the publication division of
The Astrology Center of America
207 Victory Lane, Bel Air MD 21014

on line at www.**AstroAmerica.com**

PREFACE

The rapid increase during recent years in the progress of Astrology, and the ever-growing public interest in the science, have created a demand for an introductory book on the subject containing the essential information necessary to a practical investigation of astrological claims, without being overburdened with detail. The present work is an attempt to meet this demand, and has been written with the needs of the beginner in mind throughout. My object has been to indicate and exemplify the methods to be adopted in casting and judging a horoscope, and to simplify the procedure as much as possible. This allows the student to obtain a thorough grasp of the principles involved without being embarrassed by a multitude of rules, aphorisms, exceptions, and other information, which, however helpful it may be at a later stage, is a distinct hindrance at the beginning.

The methods of judgment are nearly all exemplified upon a single horoscope in order that the different fields of influence may be better appreciated than would be the case were several maps used, but I am fortunately able to include rather more diagrams and examples than are usual in a book of this kind, and these have been selected to furnish a further insight into the planetary action in the various departments of life.

Nothing essential to the practice of Astrology has been omitted, and if I have succeeded in my object the beginner will be able to acquire with as little difficulty as possible a sound knowledge of the principles and methods of the subject and their practical application.

London.   VIVIAN E. ROBSON.

CONTENTS

PART I

HOW TO CAST A HOROSCOPE

PART II

PLANETS, SIGNS, AND HOUSES

PART III

HOW TO JUDGE A HOROSCOPE

CONTENTS

PART IV

HOW TO CALCULATE FUTURE INFLUENCES

PART I
HOW TO CAST A HOROSCOPE

CHAPTER I

THE HOROSCOPE DIAGRAM

The first step in practically all astrological work is the " casting " or calculating of a horoscope. A horoscope, or as it is often called, a map, chart, or figure, is simply an accurate map of the heavens as seen from a particular spot on the earth at a particular time. This map contains in diagrammatic form the places of the planets and signs of the Zodiac as they appear at the required moment, that is, at the moment of birth, which for astrological purposes is taken as the moment the child utters its first cry. In astrological parlance such a horoscope is called a *nativity*, and the person for whom it is cast is called the *native*.

We will begin by considering the actual diagram itself, and then the separate factors which go to complete it and make a proper horoscope of it.

There are two forms of diagram in common use, a circular one and a square one. The former is much to be recommended, and is rapidly superseding the latter, but as the square form is still frequently met with, it is as well for the student to understand it, though he will find the circular map much clearer and easier to use. These diagrams are shown in Figs. 1 and 2.

For the moment we will study Fig. 1. The small circle in the centre represents the earth, and specifically the birth-place, while the double outer circle represents the belt of the Zodiac surrounding the earth and the planets. The lines that look like spokes, which may be imagined as projecting from the earth, divide the intervening space into twelve divisions which are known as the *Mundane Houses*, or simply

3

Houses for short. The observer is supposed to be standing in the small centre circle facing towards the South, and the point on the outer double circle touched by the vertical

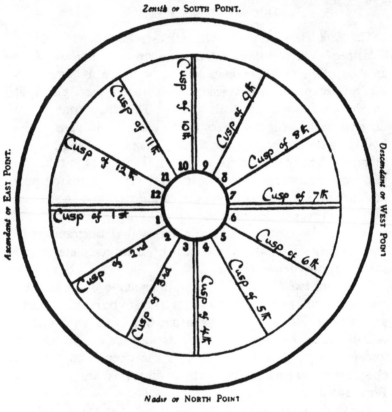

FIG. 1.

spoke marks the point overhead, or that at which the Sun and planets attain their greatest elevation above the horizon. This point is known as the Midheaven or Medium Coeli, usually abbreviated M.C. The opposite point at the bottom of the map will therefore represent the North or the point under foot, and this is known as the Imum Coeli or I.C. The vertical line joining these two points is the meridian. The horizontal line passing right across the map actually

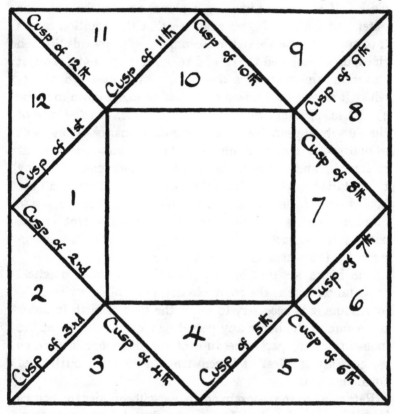

FIG. 2.

represents the horizon. As the observer is facing South, the left extremity of this line marks the East, where the Sun and planets rise, and is called the Ascendant. The point on the extreme right marks the West, where the planets set, and is called the Descendant. The earth rotates on its own axis once in twenty-four hours, and we may imagine the small centre circle, with its spokes attached to it, rotating from left to right, that is in the opposite way to the hands of a clock. If we further imagine a planet fixed in between the outer and inner circles we shall see that this rotation causes it to appear to rise above the ascendant, pass upwards through the houses numbered 12, 11, and 10, until it attains its greatest elevation, and then pass down through houses 9, 8, and 7, where it crosses the horizon again and proceeds down to house 4, and so on round to the ascendant again. In the case of the Sun its appearance on the ascendant marks the moment of sunrise ; it is on the midheaven at noon ; on the descendant at sunset ; and on the nadir, or I.C., at midnight. Thus by this rotation of the earth all the planets pass through all the houses once a day, going in a direction against the house numbers, and it will be seen that this movement is due entirely to the earth and has nothing to do with any movement by the planet on its own account.

The house position of the planets is of great practical importance, and as the complete circle occupies only twenty-four hours it is necessary to know the *time* of birth in order to be sure of the house any planet happens to occupy at the moment. Also, partly because of the difference in time as we go East or West of Greenwich, the place of birth is of equal importance.

Returning to the diagram again, we will consider the houses in rather more detail. They are numbered downwards from the ascendant, and this arrangement is invariable; the house on the left of the diagram and just below the horizon is always No. 1, the opposite one is always No. 7, and so on. Each of these houses has a distinct influence of its own. The spokes in the diagram represent the boundaries of the houses, each spoke being called the *cusp*, or beginning, of a house. The

6

left horizontal spoke, or the ascendant, is the cusp of the first house ; the next below it is the cusp of the second house, and so on as marked in Fig. 1.   The cusp should be thought of in connection with its own house only.   Thus the cusp of the first house has no relation at all to the twelfth, although it appears to divide these houses.   This is an important matter to bear in mind, because in practice the influence of a house is at its strongest on the cusp of that house, so that a planet on the cusp of, say, the fifth house is affecting matters ruled by the fifth house as strongly as it can, and is not in any way influencing fourth house matters as well, as might be supposed. Therefore we should always think of the cusps in relation to their proper houses.

So far we have ignored the square map, but the same principles hold good throughout, of course, and Fig. 2 shows the invariable arrangement of the houses and cusps in maps of that shape.

CHAPTER II

The twelve houses which we have been considering are the chief rulers over the environment of the native. Each house rules over certain of the affairs of life, and the chief influence of a planet or other heavenly body is exerted through the affairs ruled by the house in which it is situated at the moment of birth. Therefore it is essential to obtain a thorough knowledge of the influence of each house. The following list contains the chief activities of the houses, and in order to assist the student the primary and more important rulerships are printed in capitals. If these are memorised the subsidiary meanings can easily be added, for in most cases they will be found to be logical extensions of the root idea.

1st House. The NATIVE, or subject of the horoscope himself; his appearance, habits, characteristics, health, temperament, and the general way in which he looks on the world. This house is often called the Ascendant, though the term strictly applies only to the cusp.

2nd House. MONEY, movable possessions.

3rd House. RELATIVES and SHORT JOURNEYS. Brothers and sisters, cousins, neighbours. Journeys which can be completed in a day, means of communication, letters, documents, papers. In a general way it rules all relations with others.

4th House. HOME, dwelling-house, property, buildings, mines, immovable possessions ; domestic life, the beginning and also the end of life ; the father of the native.

5th House. CHILDREN and PLEASURE. Love affairs, holidays, games of chance, speculation.

8

6th House. HEALTH and sickness, food and clothing, servants, employees, pet animals.

7th House. MARRIAGE, the wife or husband, partnership and the partner, whether business or otherwise. Also the relation of the native to other people, and therefore it rules open enemies and opponents.

8th House. DEATH. Legacies, goods of the dead; also other people's money, and especially the money of the wife, husband, or business partner.

9th House. LONG JOURNEYS, voyages, travel, foreign countries; also religion, the Church, Law, books and publications, and relatives by marriage.

10th House. OCCUPATION, honour, credit, worldly standing, employers, superiors. It rules the mother of the native. This entire house is often called the Midheaven or M.C., but the term belongs properly only to the actual cusp.

11th House. FRIENDS, acquaintances, associates, societies; also hopes and aspirations.

12th House. SORROW, confinement, imprisonment, restraint in hospital, asylum or similar institution; also trouble especially self-caused, secret enmity, charity given or received.

It should be noticed that the houses below the horizon are rather more obscure or personal than those above. Thus the first rules the self, and the 7th others; the 2nd one's own money, and the 8th that of others; the 3rd short journeys, and the 9th long ones; the 4th private life, and the 10th public life; the 5th a particular friend, and the 11th acquaintances; the 6th sickness, and the 12th hospitals.

Other compound meanings can be given to each house according to its relation to the others. Thus the 8th house obtains its rulership over other people's money by its position as the 2nd (money) house from the 7th (other people).

Similarly the health of children would come under the 10th because it is the 6th from the 5th.

STRENGTH OF HOUSES

Quite apart from their rulership over the affairs of life the houses bestow more or less strength upon the planets that are found in them at birth. Certain houses are obscure and others prominent. Each is equally important in regard to the matter it rules, but not when considered simply as a twelfth part of the heavens or a kind of receptacle for a planet. In general the higher up a house is in the horoscope the more prominence it gives, rather on the principle that the highest position is " King of the Castle," but this must be taken in a wide sense. We find in practice that the houses can be classified from the point of view of strength into three groups, as follows :—

Angles or Angular Houses	1st	4th	7th	10th
Succedent Houses	2nd	5th	8th	11th
Cadent Houses	3rd	6th	9th	12th

The Angles are the houses whose cusps form the vertical and horizontal lines of the meridian and horizon. These are by far the strongest in the horoscope, and any planets situated in them act markedly upon the life. The 1st and 10th houses are the strongest of all, then comes the 7th, and lastly the 4th.

The Succedent Houses are so called because they succeed or follow the angles. Planets here tend to act strongly on the feelings and emotions, but less strongly in events than the angles.

The Cadent Houses, which are so called because they " fall away " from the angles, greatly influence the mind, but tend to obscurity in affairs. A planet in a cadent house is weak, and its influence is thereby hampered, whereas one in an angle is in a very powerful position, and its influence will be one of the dominating factors of the life.

CHAPTER III

Having grasped the nature of the horoscope diagram and its houses, we may now turn to a consideration of the planets and signs which have to be inserted in it when we come to the casting of the horoscope.

Nine heavenly bodies are utilised in astrology, namely the seven planets and the Sun and Moon. The latter are sometimes referred to as the *luminaries*, but as a rule we include them under the general term planets for the sake of convenience, though strictly neither the Sun nor the Moon is a planet, the former being the centre of our Solar System, and the latter only a satellite.

The names and symbols of the planets are as follows:—

SUN	☉	JUPITER	♃
MOON	☽	SATURN	♄
MERCURY	☿	URANUS	♅
VENUS	♀	NEPTUNE	♆
MARS	♂		

It is important to learn these symbols so thoroughly that each immediately suggests the planet's name just as the figure 2 suggests the word " two," for they and the other symbols to be learnt later are the alphabet of astrology and are in constant use.

In the above list the Sun is placed first on account of its importance, and the other planets are arranged in the order of their speed from quickest to slowest. The order from Mercury to Neptune is also that of distance from the Sun, Mercury being the nearest. It will be found convenient to

11

learn the names in the above order, and always use it when dealing with all the planets together, for unless some definite order is habitually used one is liable to miss out a planet when casting the horoscope or calculating aspects. In fact the cultivation of methodical habits in all departments of astrology will be found to be of immense help in the end.

Each of these planets has a definite influence, and rules over a great variety of things, the more important of which will be found in later chapters. It is sufficient at this stage for the student to obtain an idea of their general natures, leaving the details to be added gradually as he proceeds.

THE SUN, ⊙, has a fiery, hot and dry, positive and masculine influence. It rules honour, fame, superiors, the vitality, and constitution. In character it confers pride, dignity, nobility, generosity, ambition, ostentation, strength of will and courage.

THE MOON, ☽, is cold, moist, negative and feminine. It makes its natives changeable, imaginative, inconstant and capricious; and rules women, the public, water, and watery occupations and things. The Moon is a receptive body, and takes upon itself the nature of the sign containing it, or the planet with which it is most strongly associated in the horoscope.

MERCURY, ☿, is itself cold, dry, airy, nervous and adaptable. Like the Moon, it takes over the nature of the planet in closest association, but when uninfluenced its own nature is mental, nervous, and intellectual. It rules the mind, writing, study, travel, and messages; and it makes its natives highly strung, subtle, clever, active, restless, and talkative.

VENUS, ♀, is a *benefic* or fortunate planet, and is warm,

moist, and feminine in nature. It governs love, marriage, beauty, pleasure, the fine arts, gaiety, ornaments, and jewellery, and makes its natives gentle, refined, pleasant, affectionate, and artistic.

MARS, ♂, is a *malefic* or evil planet, and is hot, dry, fiery, forceful, positive, and masculine. It rules fire, war, passion, fevers, wounds, iron and sharp tools, and makes its natives hasty, warlike, passionate, rash, self-confident, combative, and courageous.

JUPITER, ♃, is benefic by nature and is expansive, warm, moist, and masculine. It rules churches, religion, Law and the professions generally, also sport, and brings success and protection. It makes its natives philosophical, philanthropic, humane, generous, prudent, cheerful, optimistic, sympathetic, just, and frequently lovers of sport.

SATURN, ♄, is malefic, and is cold, dry, hard, restricting, and masculine. It rules old age, sorrow, melancholy, disease and chronic ailments, misfortunes, falls, and dark things and places ; and it makes its natives cautious, secretive, jealous, miserly, acquisitive, faithful, serious, steady, and patient.

URANUS, ♅, is malefic, and is cold, spasmodic, and masculine. It rules unusual things, occupations, and people ; electrical apparatus, occultism, and sudden and catastrophic happenings. It makes its natives abrupt, ingenious, original, independent, and eccentric.

NEPTUNE, ♆, is usually malefic, sometimes extremely so, but may be highly spiritual in nature. It is warm, moist, and feminine, and rules mysticism, clairvoyance, trances and mediumship, hospitals, voyages and the sea, treachery, deceit, drugs, and produces a chaotic tendency in affairs. It makes its natives dreamy, sensuous, musical, artistic, self-indulgent, unstable, sensitive, and highly emotional.

It will be seen from the above that some planets appear to be good and others bad. Actually each planet has both good and bad sides to its nature. Thus Jupiter when operating favourably causes generosity, but when unfavourable produces reckless extravagance ; Venus may cause love or sensuality ; the Sun may be dignified or bombastic, and so with every planet. The exact way in which it will operate depends upon its position in the given horoscope. At the same time it is true that certain planets are more disposed to act favourably or unfavourably than others. Venus and Jupiter are naturally favourable, while Mars and Saturn are the reverse, so we find that the former when showing their unpleasant side are not so bad as the latter when showing theirs. Conversely Mars and Saturn can be very beneficial, but not quite to the extent possible to Venus and Jupiter.

CHAPTER IV

The planets are all revolving round the Sun at different rates, and it is therefore necessary to use some means of representing their positions relative to each other and to the earth at any given moment. The astronomer usually calculates the positions of the planets as they would be seen by an observer situated in the Sun, but for astrological purposes we need to know how the planets appear as seen from the earth, because we are dealing solely with their influence upon the earth and its inhabitants. For this reason we usually speak of the Sun as moving, because to an observer on the earth it appears to do so. The inaccuracy is in terminology only.

In order to describe the position of a planet in space it is necessary to decide upon a constant circle and fix a definite point on it to mark the beginning. We can then say that the planet is so far along the circle from this point, and so far above or below the line of the circle itself. There are two convenient circles that may be chosen for this purpose. One is the earth's equator, or rather the projection of the earth's equator into space. The beginning of this circle is fixed at the point where it is cut by the Sun's apparent path round the earth, or in other words, at the point occupied by the Sun on the 21st March every year. The circle is divided into 360 degrees (360°), each degree of which contains 60 minutes (60'), and each minute 60 seconds (60''), and the planet is said to be so many degrees, minutes, and seconds along the circle, and so many degrees, minutes and seconds above or below it. The distance along this circle is technically

15

called *Right Ascension*, usually abbreviated **R.A.**, and that above or below is called *Declination*, abbreviated Dec. We shall not need to use R.A. in our present studies, but the declination of the planet, or its distance above or below the equator, is of importance. Declination is said to be North if the planet is above the equator, and South if below it.

The second, and usual astrological method of fixing the position of a planet is along the circle of the earth's orbit, or in other words along the apparent path of the Sun round the earth. It is found that all the planets move round the Sun within a narrow band some few degrees on each side of the exact central line, which is known as the *Ecliptic*. This band is called the *Zodiac*, and as well as being divided into the usual 360°, is also divided into twelve equal parts of 30°, each called *Signs*. The beginning point of this circle is the same as that used in the case of the equator, and is the point where the equator and ecliptic intersect, and which is annually occupied by the Sun on 21st March. This point is called *0° Aries*. The distance of a planet measured along the circle from 0° Aries is called its *Longitude*, and its distance above or below the exact ecliptic line is called its *Latitude*, though this is not commonly used in astrology.

Now the longitude may be measured direct from 0° Aries in degrees, minutes, and seconds, but it is usual to measure instead in signs first, and specify the degrees in a sign rather than the degrees from the beginning point of the circle. Thus a planet distant 65° 27′ from 0° Aries would be said to be in 5° 27′ Gemini, which is the third sign, because it has passed through all the 30° of Aries, all the 30° of Taurus, and is 5° 27′ into Gemini. The reason for using the sign position in this way is that each sign possesses a distinctive influence of its own. We have already seen that a planet is radiating a certain type of influence down upon us. This influence comes down through the sign in which the planet happens to be situated, and is modified by the influence of that sign. This combined influence is then again still further modified by the house in which it is placed in the horoscope. The object of astrology is to show how to blend these influences and determine the final result.

The names and symbols of the Signs of the Zodiac are as follows :—

1. ARIES. The Ram ♈ opposite to 7. LIBRA. The Balance ♎

2. TAURUS. The Bull ♉ ,, 8. SCORPIO. The Scorpion ♏

3. GEMINI. The Twins ♊ ,, 9. SAGITTARIUS. The Archer ♐

4. CANCER. The Crab ♋ ,, 10. CAPRICORN. The Goat ♑

5. LEO. The Lion ♌ ,, 11. AQUARIUS. The Waterman ♒

6. VIRGO. The Virgin ♍ ,, 12. PISCES. The Fishes ♓

These must be learnt thoroughly in their relative order. As the Zodiac is a circle each sign falls opposite to another, as shown above, and it is necessary to know what sign is opposite to any given one.

The influence of each sign is similar to that of the corresponding house. The sign Aries normally corresponds to the 1st house, Taurus to the 2nd, and so on, no matter what sign may at any time be occupying that house. Actually the houses obtain their rulerships through correspondence with the signs, for the latter are rather more fixed and enduring. In the horoscope, a planet in Taurus will act upon money matters to some extent as if it were in the 2nd house, but the effect of the signs is stronger upon character and more per-

17

manent matters, while the houses are more concerned with environment and changing conditions.

It will be found, no matter how unlikely or absurd it may seem, that the characteristics of the signs closely resemble those of the animals whose names they bear in certain cases. Thus natives of Aries are headstrong and rush at things— just like a ram ; Taurus natives are obstinate and sometimes bull-like in appearance ; Cancer natives tend to get their hands upon something and never let go, like the crab, and moreover sometimes waddle or walk sideways ; and similarly in the case of the other signs. There are many classifications of the signs according to these characteristics which are valuable in practical astrological work. Thus the signs of those creatures that make no sound, the Crab, the Scorpion, and the Fish, are termed Mute signs, and are found to be connected with dumbness. But the most generally important classification of the signs is into groups called *Triplicities* and *Quadruplicities*. These are as follows :—

Triplicities.

Fiery Signs	♈	♌	♐
Earthy Signs	♉	♍	♑
Airy Signs	♊	♎	♒
Watery Signs	♋	♏	♓

These signs have relation to the elements whose names they bear, so that planets in watery signs, for example, tend to bring work in connection with water and are prominent in the horoscopes of sailors, barmaids, etc. Apart from this however, the Fiery signs, give an inspirational, intuitive, and spiritual bent to the nature, earthy signs are solid, practical, and material ; airy signs are mental and artistic ; and watery signs are emotional and sensational.

18

THE SIGNS OF THE ZODIAC

Quadruplicities.

Cardinal or Movable Signs	♈	♋	♎	♑
Fixed Signs	♉	♌	♏	♒
Mutable or Common Signs	♊	♍	♐	♓

The group influence of the cardinal signs is to give an active, energetic, and ambitious nature, with a pioneering spirit in some direction. The fixed signs are steady, plodding, persevering, and resist change. The mutable signs are allied to the mind, and are restless, indecisive, and nervous.

These two main divisions work in together, Thus it will be noticed that each Quadruplicity contains a sign of each element, and conversely each Triplicity contains a cardinal, a fixed, and a mutable sign. By studying this arrangement much may be learnt about the nature of each sign. We have seen that the cardinal signs give energy, but the energy of Libra will be expended largely through the mind and artistic feelings because that sign is also airy; while the energy of Capricorn will be practical and material because Capricorn is also an earthy sign.

These two classifications should be learnt very thoroughly for they are being continually used.

Only one other classification need be noticed at present. The odd signs, namely ♈, ♊, ♌, ♎, ♐, and ♒ are termed Positive or Masculine, while the even signs ♉, ♋, ♍, ♏, ♑, and ♓ are Negative or Feminine. The latter are more receptive and less forceful than the former.

19

CHAPTER V

The action of a planet in a horoscope is never entirely unmodified. Every planet affects us through the medium of the sign of the Zodiac in which it happens to posited at birth, and it therefore becomes of importance to understand not only the actual nature of that modification but also the harmony existing between the planets and signs, so that we may judge whether the influence of the planet will flow through the sign easily or whether it will be hampered.

It is found that every planet is stronger in some signs than others, according to whether their natures are harmonious or the reverse. But in addition to this we know that certain signs respond very closely to certain planets, and are influenced by those planets no matter where the latter may be situated in the horoscope. Each sign responds in this way to a particular planet, and is said to be " ruled " by that planet. This is a very important matter in practical astrology. Suppose, for example, that the second house in the horoscope is unoccupied by a planet, and we wish to judge of the financial prospects. The way in which we do this is to see what sign is on the cusp of that house and then base our judgment upon the position and aspects of the planet which *rules* that sign. A thorough knowledge of these rulerships is therefore essential.

The Sun and Moon rule one sign each, and the other planets from Mercury to Saturn rule two signs each. Uranus and Neptune have no definite rule over any sign.

20

⊙ rules   ♌

☽ rules   ♋

☿ rules ♊ and ♍

♀ rules ♉ and ♎

♂ rules ♈ and ♏

♃ rules ♐ and ♓

♄ rules ♑ and ♒

When a planet happens to occupy its own sign it becomes very strong and powerful either for good or evil, but if in one of the signs opposite to its own its action is hampered.   This position is called its *detriment*.

Another position of strength is when a planet is in its *exaltation*, when it is nearly as powerful as in its own sign. The signs of exaltation are as follows :—

⊙ is exalted in ♈

☽ is exalted in ♉

☿ is exalted in ♍

♀ is exalted in ♓

♂ is exalted in ♑

♃ is exalted in ♋

♄ is exalted in ♎

An exalted planet is powerful and at the same time rather more inclined to good than evil.   The opposite sign to the exaltation is called the *fall*, and when the planet is here it is weak and inclined to evil.

Of these positions it is of the greatest importance to be perfectly familiar with the planets' own signs.   The exaltation and fall, though important, need not be specially memorised at the moment and will be acquired by practice.   The

21

following Table gives a summary of the above positions for handy reference :—

Planet.	Rules.	Detriment.	Exaltation.	Fall.
☉	♌	♒	♈	♎
☽	♋	♑	♉	♏
☿	♊ and ♍	♐ and ♓	♍	♓
♀	♉ and ♎	♏ and ♈	♓	♍
♂	♈ and ♏	♎ and ♉	♑	♋
♃	♐ and ♓	♊ and ♍	♋	♑
♄	♑ and ♒	♋ and ♌	♎	♈

In addition to the special positions just described, every planet is more at home in some signs than others. This can be judged to a great extent by comparing the elemental natures of the sign and planet. Thus Mars is a hot and fiery planet, and is more at home in the fiery signs than in the watery, with the exception of Scorpio ; while Saturn on the other hand is dry and cold and therefore prefers the earthy signs.

MOTION THROUGH SIGNS

The Sun, Moon, and all the planets move at different rates of speed through the signs in order from Aries to Taurus and so on, passing from Pisces back into Aries again. At certain times, however, they all, with the exception of the Sun and Moon, appear to slow down, stop, and proceed backwards for a time, after which they turn and continue in the normal forward direction again. This is known as *Retrogradation*, and a planet moving backward is said to be retrograde. The backward motion is only an apparent one, for the planet never actually moves in this way, and the effect is caused by the

22

relative positions of the planet, the Sun, and ourselves. To a passenger seated in an express train which is passing another train going more slowly in the same direction, the latter has the appearance of moving backwards, and the phenomenon of retrogradation is due to a similar combination of relative positions and movements.

In the Ephemeris the day on which a planet has begun to go backwards is marked by the symbol ℞ which stands for Retrograde ; and the day on which it has finally resumed its forward motion is marked with the letter D, meaning Direct. A planet loses power by being retrograde, and is weak for either good or evil.

This movement of the planets through the signs is quite distinct from their movement through the houses of the horoscope. It will be remembered that the planets pass through the houses against the order of the houses (and signs) owing to the earth's rotation. Their own proper motion, however, is in the opposite direction to this, and very much slower. Thus we have seen that each planet goes through all the houses in a day, but by its own motion through the Zodiac it moves only a degree or so, and in most cases much less. These different motions should not be confused.

23

CHAPTER VI

As the planets are all moving through the Zodiac at different speeds they are constantly altering their positions relative to each other and to the earth. The distance between the planets as seen from the earth and measured in degrees of the Zodiac is very important for upon that depends the way in which they act upon each other. Certain distances are found to be harmonious and others evil. Thus when any two planets are 60° or 120° from each other their influences blend harmoniously, and one helps the other. But if the same two planets happen to be 90° apart the effect is very adverse, and each hinders and distorts the action of the other. These distances are called *aspects*, and their names, symbols, distances, and natures are as follows :—

	Symbol	Degrees apart	Nature
CONJUNCTION	☌	0	Variable
SEMISEXTILE	⚺	30	Weakly good
SEMISQUARE	∠	45	Weakly evil
SEXTILE	✶	60	Good
SQUARE	☐	90	Evil
TRINE	△	120	Very good
SESQUIQUADRATE or SESQUARE	⚼	135	Weakly evil
QUINCUNX	⚻	150	Doubtful, but very weak
OPPOSITION	☍	180	Very evil

24

There is also the PARALLEL, symbol P, which occurs when two planets are equal in declination, and is a very powerful and variable aspect, and similar to the conjunction.

The influence of two planets in aspect depends entirely upon the nature of the *aspect* as to whether it is good or otherwise. The sextile between any two planets is good in effect no matter what planets they may be, though of course it is correspondingly better between good planets than between evil ones. In the case of the conjunction and parallel, however, this is not so, and the effect varies according to the planets involved. A conjunction of two benefics is good, and of two malefics is bad. Thus ♀♂♃ is extremely good, and ♂♂♄ extremely bad. The conjunction of a good and a bad planet is mixed, the effect being to spoil the influence of the benefic and improve that of the malefic. The result depends largely upon the sign in which the conjunction is formed. Thus ♂♂ ♀ in ♏ is distinctly harmful to ♀ because ♂ has by far the greater power in that sign, but the same conjunction in ♎ would do ♀ little harm. This principle should be observed in all cases.

To calculate aspects simply count from one planet to the other along the shortest distance between them. Thus if the ☉ were in ♈ 10 and ♃ in ♌ 10 we should count from ♈ to ♌ as that is the shorter. There are 20° more left in ♈, then 30° for all ♉, 30° for ♊, 30° for ♋, and 10° into ♌. Adding these up we find that it comes to 120° and the aspect is therefore ☉△♃, or ♃△☉, whichever way you care to write it. This process will be more fully exemplified later.

Now for the effect to operate it is not essential for the planets to be in *exact* aspect. They may be several degrees wide. The trine is actually 120°, but the effect would also be strongly felt if the planets were only 118° apart, or if they were 122° apart. The latitude that can be allowed on each

c   25

side of the exact distance is called the *orb* of the aspect. It is difficult to give a list of exact orbs, because the effect of the aspect is strongest when exact, and gradually fades as the distance increases or decreases, so that any list of orbs should be taken as giving the approximate amounts that can be allowed to be sure that the aspect is still operative. The usual quantities that are generally agreed upon are as follows :—♂ and ☍, about 8°. If the ☉ or ☽ be one of the bodies 10° may be allowed, and if the aspect be between the ☉ and ☽ it may be extended to 12°.

△ and □. About 8°.

✳. About 7°.

∠ and ⊡. About 4°.

⚺ and ⚻. About 2°.

P. Only 1°.

Therefore the influence of the trine, for example, would begin when the planets were about 112° apart, increase in strength up to the exact 120°, and then fade gradually until the distance had increased to about 128°, when the effect would cease to be appreciable.

When one planet is overtaking another and coming towards an aspect we say it is *applying* to the aspect; and when it is leaving it we say it is *separating*. If ♃ were in ♌ 10 and the ☉ in ♈ 2, we should say that the ☉ was applying to the △ of ♃, because the ☉ is the quicker-moving body. A slow-moving body cannot either apply to or separate from a more quickly moving one. The ☽ applies to, and separates from, all the planets; ☿ to all except the ☽; ♀ to all except ☿ and the ☽; the ☉ to all except ♀, ☿, and the ☽; and so on up to ♅ which can apply only to ♆; and ♆ which cannot apply to any.

CHAPTER VII

CONVERSION OF TIME

The process of casting the horoscope is performed in two stages. First we have to find how the signs of the Zodiac are related to the birthplace at the exact moment of birth and insert them in the outer circle of the map. Then we have to find the exact position of each planet in the Zodiac, that is its exact longitude at birth, and insert them all in the houses of the diagram in accordance with the positions we have found. It is necessary to remember one important general principle, namely :—

Calculate the cusps of the houses for Local Time.
Calculate the planets' places for Greenwich Time.

We must therefore know first of all how to convert one kind of time into the other.

Greenwich Time. Greenwich Time is used for every purpose throughout the British Isles. This time is really correct in accordance with the Sun only for Greenwich and places in exactly the same longitude, but it has been found convenient to use it as a standard for the whole country. Any birth time in Great Britain may be taken as expressed in Greenwich Time. The only exception to this is when Summer Time is in force.

Local Time. This is the exact mean time correct for any particular place according to the Sun. At noon at any place the Sun is at its highest point, which we may think of as directly overhead.[1] When the Sun is overhead at Greenwich

---

[1] Astronomical students should note that it is the mean Sun which is referred to throughout. Any consideration of Apparent Time is beyond the scope of this book.

it is the moment of Greenwich noon, and as we have seen, this is also taken as noon throughout the whole country. But at this same moment of time the Sun will not be directly overhead at Cardiff, for example, for owing to the position of that place west of Greenwich the Sun will not be overhead there until some minutes later. Therefore when it is exact noon at Greenwich it is *called* noon at Cardiff also for the sake of convenience, but really by the *local* time of Cardiff it is some minutes before noon. This difference between Greenwich Time and Local Time is very easily calculated, and depends solely upon the *longitude* of the place east or west of Greenwich, which may be found in any good atlas. One degree of longitude is equivalent to 4 minutes' difference in time, and one minute of longitude is equivalent to 4 seconds in time. Therefore to find the equivalent of the longitude in time simply call the degrees and minutes of longitude minutes and seconds of time and multiply by four. Thus in the case of Cardiff we have :—

Longitude of Cardiff	3° 10'
Call this	3m 10s
Multiply by	4
	12m 40s

Therefore the equivalent in time is 12m 40s.

For Cleveland, Ohio, U.S.A., we have :—

Longitude of Cleveland	81° 39'
Call this	81m 39s
Multiply by	4
	326m 36s

That is 5h 26m 36s.

Exactly the same method is used for places east of Greenwich. Thus for Christchurch, New Zealand, we have :—

Longitude of Christchurch	..	172° 30'
Call this	..	172m 30s
Multiply by		4
		690m 0s

That is 11h 30m 0s.

Now to find the Local Time of any place the rule is as follows :—

(a) If the place is West of Greenwich—Subtract the longitude equivalent from the Greenwich Time.

(b) If the place is East of Greenwich—Add the longitude equivalent to the Greenwich Time.

Taking the above examples let us find the Local Time at each of these three places when it is 6.30 p.m. at Greenwich.

1. *Cardiff.* The longitude equivalent of this was found to be 12m 40s West.

Greenwich Time	..	6h 30m 0s p.m.
Subtract West long. equivalent ..		12 40
Local Time at Cardiff ..	..	6h 17m 20s p.m.

2. *Cleveland.* Longitude equivalent 5h 26m 36s West.

Greenwich Time	..	6h 30m 0s p.m.
Subtract longitude ..	..	5 26 36
Local Time at Cleveland ..	..	1h 3m 24s p.m.

3. *Christchurch.* Longitude equivalent 11h 30m 0s East.

Greenwich Time	..	6h 30m 0s p.m.
Add Longitude	..	11 30 0
Local Time at Christchurch	..	18h 0m 0s p.m.

29

The answer here is 18 hours after noon, which is 6 *a.m.* of the next day.   There can be no confusion if you think of what you are doing in a case like this.   You are *adding* nearly 12 hours to 6.30 p.m., and therefore your result will be round about the same time next morning.   If this longitude had been west instead of east you would have been subtracting nearly 12 hours from 6.30 p.m., and would therefore have obtained a result in the morning of the same day.   The above calculation for Christchurch means that at 6.30 p.m. on, say 1st June at Greenwich, it is 6.0 a.m. of the 2nd June at Christchurch.

Standard Time.   We have seen that Greenwich Time is used as a standard for all places in Great Britain, although it is strictly correct only for places on the same longitude as Greenwich itself.   The same principle is used all over the world, and a series of Standard Times is employed so as to keep a uniform time over large districts and avoid the inconvenience that would be caused if every place kept its own local time.   Thus that section of the United States lying between 67° 30′W and 82° 30′W longitude uses a time set at exactly five hours slow of Greenwich.   Therefore any time given us as that of a birth in that belt may be taken as registered in this kind of Standard Time, and must be converted to Greenwich Time and Local Time for astrological purposes.

To convert Standard Time into Greenwich Time :—

(*a*) Add the Standard if the place is west of Greenwich.

(*b*) Subtract the Standard if the place is east of Greenwich.

A list of the Standards in use will be found in Zadkiel's or Whitaker's Almanac for any year.

As an example let us suppose a birth is stated to have occurred at New York at 6.30 p.m.   This will be in Standard

Time.   The longitude of New York is 73° 59′W, and it therefore falls into the belt which uses a Standard of five hours
difference from Greenwich.

Then we have

Standard Time at New York	..	6h	30m	0s p.m.
Add Standard	.. .. ..	5	0	0
Greenwich Time ..	.. ..	11h	30m	0s p.m.

To obtain Local Time convert the longitude into time as
before :—

Longitude of New York ..	..	73°	59′
Call this ..	.. .. ..	73m	59s
Multiply by	.. .. ..		4
		295m	56s

That is 4h 55m 56s.

Then

Greenwich Time of birth ..	..	11h	30m	0s p.m.
Subtract W. long. ..	.. ..	4	55	56
Local Time of birth	.. ..	6h	34m	4s p.m.

Tabulate your results as follows :—

Birth time as given in Standard Time	6h	30m	0s p.m.
Equivalent in Greenwich Time ..	11h	30m	0s p.m.
Equivalent in Local Time	6h	34m	4s p.m.

All you need are the Greenwich and Local Times, which
should be carefully noted for use in subsequent calculations.

Sometimes this process involves passing from one day to
another, but a little thought will always make the matter clear.
Thus, suppose we are given the details of a birth as follows :—
18th June, 1930, 6.30 a.m., Melbourne, Victoria, Australia.
First of all look up what Standard is in use in Melbourne.
This will be found to be 10 hours.   Then find the longitude

of Melbourne, which the atlas gives as 145° 0'E.   Convert this
into time :—

Longitude of Melbourne ..		..	145°	0'
Call this	..	..	..	..	145m	0s
Multiply by	..	..	..		4
				580m	0

That is 9h 40m 0s.

Now proceed as follows :—

Standard Time of birth ..	6h	30m	0s a.m. 18 June
Subtract East Standard..	10	0	0
Greenwich Time ..	..	8h	30m	0s p.m. 17 June
Add East longitude	..	9	40	0
Local Time	..	..	6h	10m	0s a.m. 18 June

Tabulating, we have

Standard Time of birth ..	6h	30m	a.m. 18th
Greenwich Time of birth	8h	30m	p.m. 17th
Local Time of Birth	..	6h	10m	a.m. 18th

Discard the Standard Time and retain the Greenwich and
Local Times for future use.

It is easiest to add 12 hours mentally when subtracting, say,
10 hours from 6.30 a.m.   The 6.30 a.m. may be thought of as
18h 30m p.m. of the previous day.   In fact it is a good habit
to get into the use of the 24-hour clock, and count all times
from the previous noon.

Summer Time.   This is merely a special variety of Standard
Time.   During the months when it is in force subtract one
hour from all birth times as registered.   The result will be
Greenwich Time in the case of births in Great Britain, and the
normal standard time of the country in the case of foreign
births.

CHAPTER VIII

In order to be able to cast a horoscope it is necessary to procure an Ephemeris for the year of birth, and Tables of Houses for the *latitude* of the birthplace. A set of Tables of Houses covering the latitudes of all places in the British Isles is published by Raphael at 1s., and a set covering all other latitudes from 0° to 60° at 5s. These remain unchanged from year to year, and will serve for all horoscopes.[1]

The Ephemeris, which is also published at 1s. for any year from 1830 to date, is a kind of almanac for the year and gives the positions of the planets for noon, Greenwich Mean Time, for every day. On opening an Ephemeris there will be found a column headed " Sidereal Time." This is the time registered by the Sidereal Clock in an observatory at noon every day. The Sidereal day varies a little in length from the Mean day, so that Sidereal Time is about 4 minutes later each noon. Next there are a number of columns headed with the symbol of a planet and the word " Long." These columns, of which there is one for each planet, show the longitude in signs, degrees, and minutes, for noon at Greenwich each day. Another set of columns headed " Dec." show the declination of each planet in some cases for every noon and in others for alternate noons (or every third noon in the older Ephemerides). In the case of the Moon the longitude and declination are also given for midnight owing to their very rapid motion. A third set of columns headed " Lat." gives the latitude of each planet for alternate days and the Moon's latitude for every day. The Sun has no latitude, and is therefore omitted.

[1] These, and all other astrological requisites and publications, may be obtained from Mr. J. M. Watkins, 21 Cecil Court, Charing Cross Road, London, W.C.2.

Finally a single column headed " ☽ Node " gives the longitude of one of the points where the Moon's orbit crosses the ecliptic. This is the Moon's North Node, Caput Draconis, or the Dragon's Head (symbol ☊). The South Node, Cauda Draconis, or the Dragon's Tail (symbol ☋) is exactly opposite in longitude. The influence of these points need not be considered by the beginner, and the only columns with which he need concern himself are those of Sidereal Time, Longitude, and Declination.

The method of casting a horoscope is extremely simple, and the first section is as follows :—

1. Work out the Greenwich Time and Local Time of birth as explained in the last chapter.

2. Take out of the Ephemeris the Sidereal Time at the noon previous to birth.

3. Add to this the time that elapsed between this noon and the moment of birth expressed in Local Time.

4. Finally add a correction at the rate of 10 seconds for every hour of this time elapsed. (Actually the correction is 9.86 secs. per hour, but the difference is trifling. Its object is to convert the Mean Time elapsed into Sidereal Time.)

The result of all this is called the Sidereal Time at birth, from which we can see how the signs are arranged round the horoscope. Let us get this section settled first.

We will take an easy case to start with, and suppose a birth took place on 26th May, 1930, at 6 p.m., in London.

As the birth is in London the Greenwich and Local times are the same, and our tabulation of the birth times gives us :—

        Greenwich Time of birth 6h om os p.m. 26th
        Local Time of birth   6h om os p.m. 26th

Now the noon previous to this is noon on the 26th itself Turn to the Ephemeris for 1930 and look up 26th May.

Against this date in the column headed " Sidereal Time "
will be found 4h 13m 19s. Put this down.

The time elapsed, using the Local Time of birth, between noon
on the 26th and the moment of birth, namely 6h 0m 0s p.m.
on the 26th, is 6h 0m 0s. Then we have :—

Sidereal Time previous noon ..	4h 13m 19s
Add Local Time elapsed to birth..	6h 0m 0s
Add correction at 10 secs. per hour	0h 1m 0s
Sidereal Time at birth	10h 14m 19s

Now take the Tables of Houses for the nearest latitude to
that of the birthplace. The longitude of the place is not
considered in choosing the correct Tables to use, and Tables
for any given latitude are correct for all places in that
latitude in any part of the world. There is a set of Tables
of Houses for the exact latitude of London, and we therefore
turn to these.

These Tables occupy two pages, and there are six small
Tables on each page. Looking at the top left-hand side of
the first page you will see a column headed " Sidereal Time,"
and below columns of hours, minutes, and seconds,
which advance from 0h 0m 0s to 1h 51m 38s. This column
is continued in the next Table in the centre third of the top
half of the page, and in succeeding Tables until it reaches
24h 0m 0s at the bottom right Table on the right-hand page.
Following this column of Sidereal Times in each Table will
be found six columns headed " 10," " 11," " 12," " Ascen,"
" 2," " 3." These numbers refer to the cusps of the houses.
The column headed " 10 " refers to the cusp of the 10th house,
that headed " 11 " to the cusp of the 11th house, and so on.
Under each of these comes a sign of the Zodiac, and then,
level with the various Sidereal Times, a column of numbers.

The sign at the top of the column is the sign that occupies the cusp of the house in question, and the numbers below are the degrees of that sign. Sometimes the degrees in a column get to 29 or 30, and a new sign appears in the column itself. This sign replaces the one at the head and is to be used instead for all entries below it.

In our example we found the Sidereal Time at birth to be 10h 14m 19s. Turn to the Tables of Houses for London and look down the columns headed "Sidereal Time" until you find the entry nearest in value to our above result. The column of Sidereal Time in the bottom right hand section of the left-hand page will be seen to start at 10h 8m 22s. The next entry is 10h 12m 11s, and the next 10h 15m 59s. Our Sidereal Time at birth lies in between the second and third of these and is actually nearer to the third.

Now against Sidereal Time 10h 15m 59s in the Tables we find a 2 in the column headed 10 and ♍. This means that ♍ 2° is on the cusp of the 10th house. Next to that comes a 4 in the column headed 11 and ♎. Therefore ♎ 4° is on the cusp of the 11th house. Continuing in the same way we have ♎ 27° on the 12th, ♏ 14° 53' on the Ascendant or 1st, ♐ 15° on the 2nd, and finally ♑ 22° on the 3rd.[1]

Tabulating the results we have :—

10th	..	♍	2
11th	..	♎	4
12th	..	♎	27
Asc.	..	♏	14.53
2nd	..	♐	15
3rd	..	♑	22

[1] The above entries are taken from Raphael's Tables of Houses for Great Britain. There are slight discrepancies between these and the Tables at the end of the Ephemeris, and those in the book of Tables should always be used in preference to the latter.

Instead of being content to take the values corresponding to the nearest Sidereal Time in the Tables, the student may, if he wishes to obtain greater accuracy, find the values for

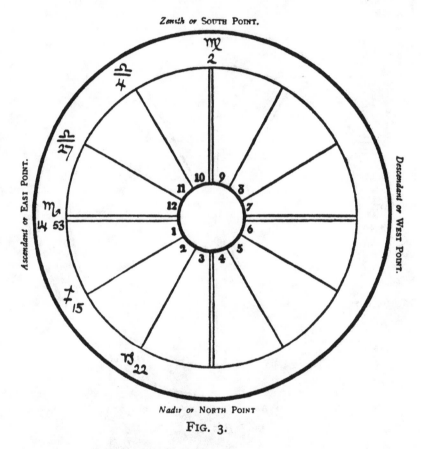

FIG. 3.

the exact Sidereal Time at birth by proportion. Thus for Sidereal Time 10h 12m 11s the 10th cusp is ♍ 1° 0', and for 10h 15m 59s it is ♍ 2° 0'. A simple Rule-of-Three sum will show what it is for any intermediate Sidereal Time. In our example the exact longitude of the 10th cusp comes to ♍ 1° 34'. The 10th cusp always moves exactly one degree between each two Sidereal Times in the Tables, and the

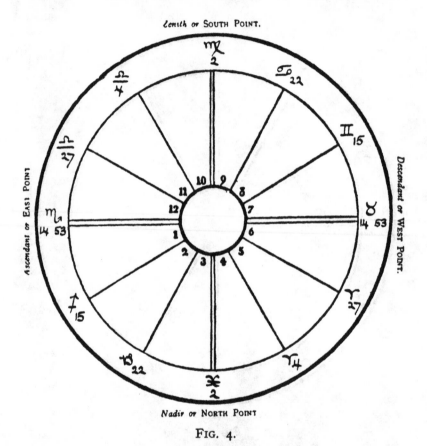

FIG. 4.

ascendant, as will be seen, moves either more or less than this amount. The proportion should be calculated only for these two cusps, for the others do not advance regularly like the 10th. For ordinary purposes, however, it is quite sufficient to use the values as they stand against the nearest Sidereal Time in the Tables.

Having tabulated the results the next step is to draw a horoscope diagram and insert these signs and degrees on their appropriate cusps as in Fig. 3.

This completes half the circle. To finish it off write down the *same degree* of the *opposite sign* on the opposite cusp.

Thus ♍ 2 is on the 10th cusp, and we therefore write ♓ 2 on the cusp of the 4th, because ♓ is opposite to ♍, as will be seen by reference to the list of signs on p. 17. After a time you will be able to write in these cusps at sight, but it may help at first to tabulate them thus :—

10th	..	♍ 2	4th	..	♓	2
11th	..	♎ 4	5th	..	♈	4
12th	..	♎ 27	6th	..	♈	27
Asc.	..	♏ 14.53	7th	..	♉	14.53
2nd	..	♐ 15	8th	..	♊	15
3rd	..	♑ 22	9th	..	♋	22

Now complete the map as in Fig. 4.

After you have got so far start with ♈ on the circle and see whether every sign is represented. You will often find that two or more are missing. In this case ♈, ♉, ♊, and ♋ are present, but after ♋ on the 9th cusp comes ♍ on the 10th, and ♌ is apparently missed out. Whenever this happens insert the missing sign in the middle of the rim between the cusps in the position it occupies according to the order of the signs. Go on round the map and see if any others are omitted. You will find that if one is omitted, the sign opposite to it is also omitted. Sometimes there are several to be inserted in this way. The final result will be as in

Fig. 5. Such signs are termed *Intercepted,* and their interception is due to the fact that the Zodiac is oblique to the earth and therefore appears to be stretched out in some places and compressed in others.

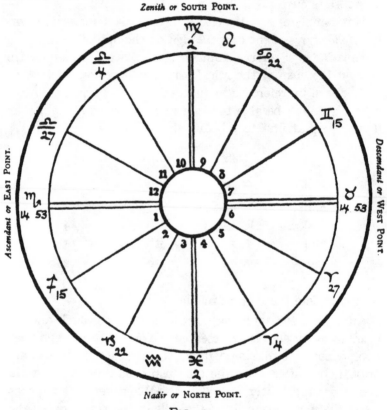

Zenith or SOUTH POINT.

Nadir or NORTH POINT.

FIG. 5.

Now the meaning of what you have done so far is this. You have found that 2° of the sign ♍ was exactly overhead at birth, and that 14° 53′ of ♏ was exactly rising on the eastern horizon. These degrees are the exact points of the Zodiac cut by the cusps of the houses. The 10th cusp cuts the Zodiac at ♍ 2, and the 11th cusp at ♎ 4. Therefore the 10th house contains 32° of the Zodiac in it. There is no jump from ♍ 2 to ♎ 4. If we imagine ourselves as walking from the 10th cusp to the 11th we should pass ♍ 3, ♍ 4, ♍ 5, and so on up to ♍ 29, then ♎ 0, ♎ 1, ♎ 2, ♎ 3, and finally when we got to ♎ 4 we should be exactly on the 11th cusp. The same remarks apply to houses with intercepted signs also. The 9th cusp cuts ♋ 22, and our walk to the 10th cusp from there would take us over ♋ 23, ♋ 24, and so on to ♋ 29, then ♌ 0, ♌ 1, and so on to ♌ 29, and finally over ♍ 0, and ♍ 1 to ♍ 2. This house therefore contains the remaining 8° of ♋, all 30° of ♌, and 2° of ♍, or in other words 40° altogether.

The Planets.

Now let us turn to the second step in casting a horoscope, and find the longitude of the planets. For this we need the Greenwich Time of birth—6 p.m., 26th May, 1930.

Turn to the Ephemeris for 1930 again and open it at the page for May. This time we are concerned with the columns headed " Long." which gives the longitude of the planets at noon, Greenwich time, every day. What we want, however, is their longitude at 6 p.m. on the 26th. Let us take the column headed " ☉ Long." first. Take out the longitude on the noon before birth and the noon after, thus :

☉ Long. noon   before birth (26th) ..   4° 29′ 48″ ♊

☉   ,,   ,,   after   birth (27th) ..   5° 27′ 25″ ♊

This means that during the 24 hours from noon on the 26th to noon on the 27th the ☉ has moved from 4° 29′ 48″ ♊ to 5° 27′ 25″ ♊. We want to know where it had got to at 6 p.m., which is 6 hours after noon on the 26th. To do this first find out exactly how far it moved in the whole 24 hours by subtracting the lesser value from the greater.

⊙ Noon 27th ..   ..   5° 27′ 25″ ♊
⊙ ,,   26th ..   ..   4° 29′ 48″ ♊
               Distance moved   0° 57′ 37″

Then say : if the ⊙ moves 0° 57′ 37″ in 24 hours, how far will it move in 6 hours ? As 6 hours is exactly a quarter of 24, it will obviously move a quarter of 0° 57′ 37″, which is 0° 14′ 24″. The ⊙ is increasing in longitude from the 26th to the 27th, so it will have advanced this amount by 6 p.m. Therefore :

⊙ Long. noon 26th ..   ..   4° 29′ 48″ ♊
Add distance moved in 6h   ..   0° 14′ 24″

⊙ Long. at 6 p.m. on 26th   ..   4° 44′ 12″ ♊

This is the general principle covering all cases. We will complete the other planets and the horoscope before passing to rather more complicated examples.

Take the ☽ next. The beginner will be well advised to omit the seconds of longitude in the case of both the ⊙ and ☽, and work to the nearest minute. We have :—

☽ at noon 27th   ..   ..   25° 51′ ♉
Subtract ☽ at noon 26th   ..   12   7 ♉

     Distance moved   ..   13   44

One quarter of this is 3° 26′.

The ☽ is advancing, so that this amount must be added to its place at noon on the 26th.

☽ at noon 26th   ..   ..   12°   7′ ♉
Add motion for 6 hours   ..   3   26

☽ at birth   15   33 ♉

Mercury comes next, and if we look at the column containing

its longitude we shall see a little ℞ in the column which
indicates that on the day against which it appears (in this
case the 9th) it has begun to move backwards, or turn
retrograde, in which direction it continues until a D appears
(in this case on 3rd June). By looking down the column we
can see that the longitude is getting less instead of increasing.
Now this means that from noon on the 26th to noon on the
27th the longitude is diminishing, so that the motion for
6 hours must be *subtracted* from the noon place on the 26th.
Otherwise the procedure is the same.

☿ at noon 26th	25° 10′ ♉ ℞
☿ at noon 27th	24 47 ♉ ℞
Distance moved ..	0 23

One quarter of this is 0° 6′ nearly.

Then ☿ at noon 26th ..	25° 10′ ♉ ℞
Subtract motion for 6 hours ..	0 6
☿ at birth	25 4 ♉ ℞

FOR VENUS

♀ at noon 27th	2° 48′ ♋
♀ at noon 26th	1 35 ♋
Distance moved ..	1 13

One quarter of this is 0° 18′. Then :

♀ at noon 26th	1° 35′ ♋
Add motion for 6 hours ..	0 18
♀ at birth	1 53 ♋

FOR MARS

♂ at noon 27th	25° 2′ ♈
♂ at noon 26th	24 17 ♈
Distance moved ..	0 45

One quarter of this is 0° 11'. Then :

♂ at noon 26th	24° 17' ♈
Add motion for 6 hours ..	0 11
♂ at birth	24 28 ♈

FOR JUPITER

♃ at noon 27th	23° 4' ♊
♃ at noon 26th	22 50 ♊
Distance moved ..	0 14

One quarter of this is 0° 3'.

♃ at noon 26th	22° 50' ♊
Add motion for 6 hours ..	0 3
♃ at birth	22 53 ♊

FOR SATURN

Saturn is also retrograde, so the motion for 6 hours must be subtracted.

♄ at noon 26th	10° 56' ♑ ℞
♄ at noon 27th	10 53 ♑ ℞
Distance moved ..	0 3

One quarter of this is 0° 1' nearly.

♄ at noon 26th	10° 56' ♑ ℞
Subtract motion for 6 hours	0 1
♄ at birth	10 55 ♑ ℞

The remaining planets ♅ and ♆ move so slowly that they have not appreciably altered their positions in 6 hours, so we may put down the positions for noon on the 26th as they stand, namely, ♅ in 14° 10' ♈ and ♆ in 0° 51' ♍.

Now tabulate all the results thus :—

⊙— 4° 44′ ♊
☽—15° 33′ ♉
☿—25° 4′ ♉ ℞
♀— 1° 53′ ♋
♂—24° 28′ ♈
♃—22° 53′ ♊
♄—10° 55′ ♑ ℞
♅—14° 10′ ♈
♆— 0° 51′ ♍

The next step is to insert these into the horoscope. Look at the ⊙ first of all. It is in 4° 44′ ♊. Now turning to the map (Fig. 5) we see that ♊ 15 is on the 8th cusp, and therefore the ⊙ must come on one side or the other of this cusp. To settle which side think of how the signs run. The 7th cusp is ♉ 14, and if we walk round the map as before we get to ♉ 15, ♉ 16, and so on. Clearly we shall reach ♊ 4° 44′ before we get to ♊ 15 on the 8th cusp. Therefore the ⊙ must be inserted in the 7th house. The best plan is to write each planet close alongside the cusp bearing the same sign, and make no attempt to show that it is perhaps many degrees distant from that cusp. You will soon get used to this, and by so doing will avoid all mistakes as to the sign the planet is in. In the case of planets in intercepted signs, write them along the inner rim of the wheel, as shown in some of the example charts (see ♅ in Fig. 7). Also do not turn the map round when writing in the planets and signs so that they appear to be standing on their heads. There is no need to do so, and it makes the maps much more difficult to read.

The ☽ is in ♉ 15° 33′. We met this point in our last walk just after we left the 7th cusp, so the ☽ must be written along the 7th cusp and just above it. Mercury in ♉ 25° 4′ is a little

45

further beyond the ☽, and is written next to it. Proceed in the same way with all the planets until you have completed the map, which will then be as shown in Fig. 6.

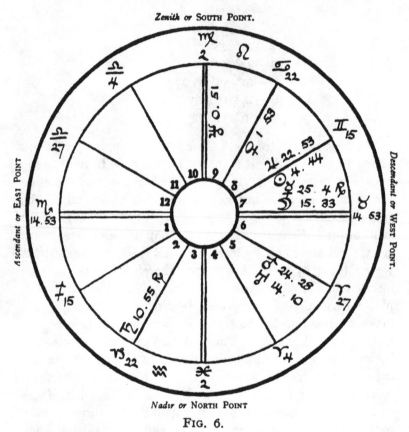

FIG. 6.

Example 2.

As a second example let us suppose a birth took place on 10th February, 1930, at 7.33 a.m., at Liverpool.

Start systematically by settling the Greenwich and Local Times. The atlas tells us that Liverpool is in latitude

53° 25′ N, and longitude 2° 59′ W. Convert the longitude into time as previously explained :—

Longitude of Liverpool ..	2°	59′
Call this	2m	59s
Multiply by		4
	11m	56s

Then :—

Greenwich Time of birth ..	7h	33m	0s a.m.
Subtract West longitude ..		11	56
Local Time of birth	7h	21m	4s a.m.

Tabulating, we get :

Local Time of birth ..	7h	21m	4s a.m. 10th
Greenwich Time of birth	7h	33m	0s a.m. 10th

For the Sidereal Time at birth and the cusps :—

Sidereal Time at previous noon (9th)	21h	15m	25s
Add Local Time elapsed	19	21	4
Add correction at 10 secs. per hour		3	13
Sidereal Time at birth	16	39	42

Note that the time elapsed is 19h odd and not 7h odd, because 7.21 a.m. on the 10th is 19h 21m after noon on the 9th. This point needs care, as it is easy to make a mistake.

Turn to the Tables of Houses for the latitude of Liverpool and look up the nearest Sidereal Time. It is 16h 37m 42s, and gives the following cusps :—

10th	♐	11
11th	♐	28
12th	♑	15
Asc.	♒	12.32
2nd	♓	17
3rd	♉	20

Fill in the same degrees of opposite signs on the other cusps, thus obtaining :—

10th	..	♐ 11	4th	..	♊ 11
11th	..	♐ 28	5th	..	♊ 28
12th	..	♑ 15	6th	..	♋ 15
Asc.	..	♒ 12.32	7th	..	♌ 12.32
2nd	..	♓ 17	8th	..	♍ 17
3rd	..	♉ 20	9th	..	♏ 20

Insert these in the diagram and fill in the intercepted signs. You will find that ♈ is intercepted in the 2nd house, and ♎ in the 8th. The cusps should now be as in Fig. 7.

The planets have to be calculated for Greenwich Time, which is 7.33 a.m. on 10th February, 1930. This is not an exact fraction of the 24 hours, and it will be found easier to work by logarithms. On the very last page of the Ephemeris will be found a Table headed " Proportional Logarithms for finding the Planets' Places," with an example of its use.

The rule is :—

1. Find the number of hours and minutes between the Greenwich time of birth and the *nearest* noon.

2. Look up the logarithm of this in the Table.

3. Find the daily motion of the planet whose position is required by subtracting its longitude on the noon before birth from that on the noon after birth (or vice versa if it is retrograde).

4. Find the log. of this and add it to the log. of the time found in Rule 2.

5. Find the degrees and minutes to which the resulting log. corresponds. This will be the planet's motion for the

required time, and it must be applied to its longitude at the nearest noon.

6. If birth was a.m., subtract the motion from its noon position, and if birth was p.m., add it. If the planet is retrograde reverse this rule—add for a.m. and subtract for p.m.

Now in our example (7.33 a.m., 10th February) the nearest noon is that of the 10th, and birth took place 4h 27m before this. The log. of 4h 27m is .7318, and this must be noted as it is used for all the planets.

The ☉ moves from ♒ 20° 2′ on the 9th to ♒ 21° 2′ on the 10th. Subtracting one from the other we get 1° 0′ for the motion in the day. Then :—

```
Log. 4h 27m    ..      ..      ..      ..    .7318
Add Sun's daily motion, log.      ..    1.3802
                                        ─────────
                                        2.1120
```

which is the log. of 0° 11′.

As the time was a.m., or before the nearest noon, this must be subtracted to obtain the Sun's place at birth.

```
☉ at noon 10th      ..      ..    21°  2′ ♒
Subtract motion for 4h 27m..       0  11
                                  ─────────
☉ at birth    ..      ..      ..   20  51 ♒
```

Next the Moon.

```
☽ at noon 10th      ..      ..    10° 31′ ♋
☽ at noon  9th      ..      ..    25  48 ♊
                                  ─────────
      Daily motion  ..      ..    14  43
```

When passing from one sign to another in the proper order

of the signs, as in this case, add 30° to allow of subtraction.
Thus 10° 31′ ♋ is equivalent to 40° 31′ ♊. This is frequently
necessary in the case of the ☽.

Log. of 4h 27m	..	.7318
Add log. of Moon's daily motion	..	.2124
		.9442

which is the log. of 2° 44′. Then :—

☽ at noon 10th	10°	31′ ♋
Subtract motion for 4h 27m..	2	44
☽ at birth	7	47 ♋

In the case of the ☽ rather more accuracy may be obtained
by taking the motion for the half-day and multiplying it by
2, but the beginner need not bother with this at present.

FOR MERCURY

☿ at noon 10th	25°	27′ ♑
☿ at noon 9th	24	45 ♑
Daily motion	0	42
Log. of 4h 27m..		.7318
Add log. of daily motion ..		1.5351
		2.2669

which is the log. of 0° 8′. Then :—

☿ at noon 10th	25°	27′ ♑
Subtract motion for 4h 27m	0	8
☿ at birth	25	19 ♑

If you continue in this way for each of the planets you will
obtain the following results :—

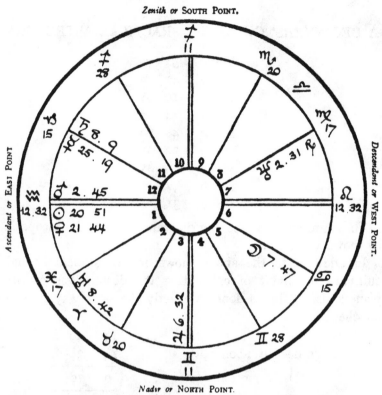

PLANET	LAT	DECL		ASPECTS								
				☉	☽	☿	♀	♂	♃	♄	♅	♆
SUN		14 S 33	☉		⊔		♂P			∠	∠	
MOON	27 N 37		☽			⊔				⚺	☍	□	✳
MERCURY	19 S 51		☿					♂P	⊔				
VENUS	15 S 31		♀							∠	∠	
MARS	20 S 31		♂						△P		✳	⊼
JUPITER	20 N 52		♃							⊼	✳	□
SATURN	22 S 27		♄								□	△
URANUS	2 N 51		♅									
NEPTUNE	11 N 12		♆									
ASCDT			ASC.									
M C			M.C.									

FIG. 7.—GENERAL EXAMPLE.

51

⊙—20° 51′ ♒

☽— 7 47 ♋

☿—25 19 ♑

♀—21 44 ♒

♂— 2 45 ♒

♃— 6 32 ♊

♄— 8 9 ♑

♅— 8 42 ♈

♆— 2 31 ♍ ℞

These are entered into the diagram, and the horoscope is as shown in Fig. 7.

In addition to the above, however, the student should cultivate the habit of calculating the declinations of the planets also. This is done in exactly the same way. Thus for the Sun :—

Sun's dec. at noon 9th	..	14°	49′ S
Sun's dec. at noon 10th	..	14	29 S
Daily motion ..	..	0	20
Log. of 4h 27m ..	..	..	.7318
Add log. of daily motion	..	..	1.8573
			2.5891

which is the log. of 0° 4′.

Now notice whether the declination is increasing or decreasing between the two noons. From the 9th to the 10th it is decreasing. Therefore at 4h 27m before noon on the 10th its value will be greater than at noon, so we must *add* the motion to the declination at noon on the 10th.

Sun's dec. at noon 10th	..	14°	29′ S
Add motion for 4h 27m	..	0	4
Sun's dec. at birth ..	..	14	33 S

By an exactly similar method we arrive at the declinations of the other bodies as follows :—

$$
\begin{array}{rrl}
\odot\text{—}14° & 33' & S \\
\mathbb{D}\text{—}27 & 37 & N \\
\text{☿}\text{—}19 & 51 & S \\
\text{♀}\text{—}15 & 31 & S \\
\text{♂}\text{—}20 & 31 & S \\
\text{♃}\text{—}20 & 52 & N \\
\text{♄}\text{—}22 & 27 & S \\
\text{♅}\text{—}\ 2 & 51 & N \\
\text{♆}\text{—}11 & 12 & N \\
\end{array}
$$

Note that the declinations of ♃, ♄, ♅, and ♆ are only given for every alternate noon, so that it is necessary to divide the motion between dates by 2 in order to obtain the daily motion. In most cases, however, the declinations of these planets can be estimated at sight owing to their very slow motion.

This is the whole process of casting a horoscope, and if you remember always to use Local Time for cusps and Greenwich Time for planets, no matter where the birth may be, you will experience no difficulty in the erection of foreign horoscopes.

In the foregoing examples the student has been taken through the actual process step by step. After he has a clear idea of the methods, however, he may appreciate a tabulated list of rules covering all cases, for nothing is more annoying than having to search here and there to find just when and how some small correction has to be used.

The following rules should be applied in order. The method to be adopted in dealing with horoscopes for South latitudes is included, but has not been exemplified as the principle is in no way different.

RULES FOR CASTING A HOROSCOPE

1. If birth is in Summer Time subtract 1 hour to obtain Greenwich Time, or normal Standard Time in the case of a foreign birth.

2. If birth is in Standard Time, add the Standard to the given time if the place is West of Greenwich. Subtract the Standard if the place is East. This gives the Greenwich Time.

3. Find the longitude of the place and convert it into time by calling the degrees of longitude minutes of time, and the minutes of longitude seconds of time, and multiplying by 4.

4. To find Local Time subtract the longitude in time from the Greenwich Time of birth if the place is West of Greenwich. Add the longitude in time if the place is East.

5. Take from the Ephemeris the Sidereal Time at the noon previous to birth.

6. If the birthplace is far distant from Greenwich take the longitude of the place in time and allow 10 secs. (9.86s exactly) for every hour, and a proportion for the minutes. Add this correction (*not* the long. itself) to the noon Sidereal Time if the place is West of Greenwich. Subtract it if East.

7. To the result add the Local Time elapsed from the previous noon to the moment of birth.

8. For this time elapsed allow 10 secs. (9.86s exactly) for every hour and a proportion for the minutes. Add this correction to the result obtained in Rule 7. The final result is the Sidereal Time at birth.

9. Turn to the Tables of Houses for the latitude of the place of birth, or the nearest latitude if exact Tables are not available. Note that *latitude* only needs to be considered in the matter, and longitude does not enter into it. Thus

Tables for New York (lat. 40° 43′ N) will serve for Rome (lat. 41° 53′ N) as they are on nearly the same latitude.

Look up the Sidereal Time in the Tables nearest to that obtained by Rule 8, and take out the corresponding cusps. Or if preferred work the 10th and 1st cusps out exactly by proportion.

10. Fill in the remaining cusps by writing in the same degrees of opposite signs on the opposite cusps.

11. Take the Greenwich Time of birth and find the number of hours and minutes it is distant from the nearest noon. Find the log. of this from the Table at the end of the Ephemeris.

12. Take from the Ephemeris the longitudes of the planets for the noon before and the noon after birth, and by subtracting one from the other find the daily motion of each planet.

13. Add the log. of the time as found in Rule 11 to the log. of the daily motion in the case of each planet. The result is the log. of the distance it has moved in the required time. Find what this is from the Table.

14. *If the planet is direct.* Add this distance to the longitude at the nearest noon if birth was p.m. Subtract it if birth was a.m.

If the planet is retrograde. Subtract this distance from the longitude at the nearest noon if birth was p.m. Add it if birth was a.m.

15. Insert the planets in the horoscope diagram in their proper positions.

16. Take the declinations and find the daily motion of each just as in the case of the longitudes (Rule 12).

17. Find the motion for the required time in the same way as in Rule 13, using declination instead of longitude.

18. *If declination is increasing.* Add the result to the

declination at the nearest noon in a p.m. birth. Subtract it in an a.m. birth.

If declination is decreasing. Subtract the result from the declination at the nearest noon in a p.m. birth. Add it in an a.m. birth.

TO CAST A HOROSCOPE FOR A PLACE IN SOUTH LATITUDE

I. Follow Rules 1 to 8 inclusive in the previous instructions.

II. To the Sidereal Time at birth obtained in Rule 8 add 12 hours (subtracting 24 hours from the sum if it exceeds that amount).

III. Use Tables of Houses for the same latitude North as the birthplace is South. Thus for lat. 52° S use Tables for 52° N.

IV. Look up the Sidereal Time obtained in Rule II and extract the cusps in the usual way.

V. Write on the diagram the same degrees but the *opposite* signs. Thus if the Tables give ♍ 2 on the 10th cusp write down ♓ 2 on the 10th, and similarly with the other cusps. Complete the remaining cusps in the usual way by writing in the same degree of the opposite signs.

VI. Calculate the planets' places and declinations for the Greenwich time of birth exactly as in Rules 11 to 18 of the previous instructions.

CHAPTER IX

CALCULATING THE ASPECTS

For the purpose of exemplifying the calculation of aspects we will take the horoscope shown in Fig. 7. First of all I should like to emphasise the fact that aspects are counted in degrees of the Zodiac from one planet to another. They are *not* in any way connected with, or dependent upon, the houses. One of the most frequent mistakes made by the beginner is due to confusion upon this point. He sees a planet in the 10th house and another in the 1st, and because they are, or appear to be, three houses apart he concludes they are in square. Certainly they may be, but they may also be in trine or in sextile. It all depends upon the number of degrees of the Zodiac between them, no matter in what houses they fall.

In calculating aspects follow the usual order of the planets beginning with the Sun, and work systematically. As all aspects are included in 180° they must be measured in the order of the signs along the shortest distance between the two planets.

☉ *and* ☽. Starting with the ☉, we look first to see whether there is any aspect between that planet and the ☽, which comes next in order. The shortest distance in the order of the signs is from the ☉ round to the ☽. The ☉ is in ♒ 20° 51′, and the ☽ in ♋ 7° 47′. For the sake of simplicity let us take each to the nearest degree, calling the ☉ ♒ 21° and the ☽ ♋ 8°. The beginner may find it less confusing to discard the odd minutes, and as each aspect has a considerable orb there will be no loss of accuracy.

Now from ♒ 21 to the end of that sign there are 9°. Beyond that we have 30° for all ♓, 30° for all ♈, 30° for all ♉, 30° for all ♊, and finally 8° of ♋ to bring us to the place of the ☽. Adding all these up we find the total distance amounts to 137°.

Another method of counting may be found easier. From ♒ 21 to ♓ 21 is 30°; from ♓ 21 to ♈ 21 is another 30°, making 60°; from ♈ 21 to ♉ 21 is another 30°, making 90°; from ♉ 21 to ♊ 21 is another 30°, making 120°. Then from ♊ 21 to ♊ 30, or ♋ 0, which is the same thing, is 9°, making 129°, and from ♋ 0 to ♋ 8 is another 8°, making a total of 137°.

Look in the list of aspects on page 24 to see if there is any recognised aspect of about this value. We find that the sesquiquadrate or sesquare is an aspect of 135°, and has an orb of about 4°. As our value of 137° is only 2° away from the exact aspect it follows that the ☉ and ☽ are in sesquare to one another, and we write down ☉ ⚼ ☽.

☉ *and* ☿. The shortest distance in this case, always measuring along the proper order of the signs, is from ☿ to the ☉. It does not matter from which planet you count so long as you measure in the order of the signs. Here ☿ is in ♑ 25 and the ☉ in ♒ 21. From ♑ 25 to ♑ 30 is 5°. From ♑ 30 (or ♒ 0) to ♒ 21 is 21°, making a total of 26°. Alternatively you may say :—From ♑ 25 to ♒ 25 is 30°. The ☉ is 4° short of ♒ 25, and therefore the distance will be 26°. The nearest aspect in the list is the semisextile of 30°. But our value is 4° off this, and only 2° are allowed as orb. Therefore the ☉ and ☿ are not in aspect.

☉ *and* ♀. These two bodies are obviously only just about 1° apart and are therefore in conjunction. Write down ☉ ☌ ♀.

☉ *and* ♂. The count is from ♂ in ♒ 3 to the ☉, a distance of 18°, which is no aspect.

☉ *and* ♃. ♃ is in ♊ 7, and the count is from the ☉. From ♒ 21 to ♓ 21 is 30°; from ♓ 21 to ♈ 21 is another 30°, making 60°; from ♈ 21 to ♉ 21 is another 30°, making 90°. Then from ♉ 21 to the end of ♉ is 9°, making 99°; and from ♊ 0 to ♊ 7 is 7°, making a total of 106°, which is not near to any aspect.

☉ *and* ♄. The count is from ♄ in ♑ 8. ♑ 8 to ♒ 8 is 30°; ♒ 8 to ♒ 21 is 13°, making a total of 43°. This is within orbs of the semisquare of 45°. Write down ☉ ∠♄.

☉ *and* ♅. The count is from the ☉ to ♅ in ♈ 9. ♒ 21 to ♓ 21 is 30°; ♓ 21 to the end of ♓ is 9°, making 39°; and another 9° into ♈ makes a total of 48°. This is also within orbs of the semisquare, so write down ☉ ∠♅.

☉ *and* ♆. The count is from ♆ in ♍ 3. ♍ 3 to ♎ 3 is 30°; ♎ 3 to ♏ 3 another 30°, making 60°; ♏ 3 to ♐ 3, 90°; ♐ 3 to ♑ 3, 120°; ♑ 3 to ♒ 3, 150°; and finally ♒ 3 to ♒ 21 is 18°, making the total 168°, which is no aspect.

This completes the aspects formed by the ☉, and the ☽ is the next planet on the list.

☽ *and* ☿. This is the first pair to be examined. The nearest distance between ☿ in ♑ 25 and the ☽ in ♋ 8 is from ☿ to the ☽. Then ♑ 25 to ♒ 25 is 30°; ♒ 25 to ♓ 25, 60°; ♓ 25 to ♈ 25, 90°; ♈ 25 to ♉ 25, 120°; ♉ 25 to ♊ 25, 150°; ♊ 25 to the end of ♊, 5°, making 155°; and ♋ 0 to ♋ 8 is 8°, making the total 163°. This is no aspect.

☽ *and* ♀. The count is from ♀ in ♒ 22. To ♓ 22 is 30°; to ♈ 22 is 60°; to ♉ 22, 90°; to ♊ 22, 120°. Then 8° more in ♊ and 8° in ♋ bring the total to 136°. This is within 1° of the exact sesquare, so write down ☽ ⚼ ♀.

Continuing in this manner we obtain the following results:—

☽ and ♂ .	155°	No aspect		☿ and ♃ .	132°	☿⚼♃
☽ and ♃ .	31°	☽⚹♃		☿ and ♄ .	17°	No aspect
☽ and ♄ .	180°	☽☍♄		☿ and ♅ .	74°	No aspect
☽ and ♅ .	89°	☽□♅		☿ and ♆ .	142°	No aspect
☽ and ♆ .	55°	☽⚹♆		♀ and ♂ .	19°	No aspect
☿ and ♀ .	27°	No aspect		♀ and ♃ .	105°	No aspect
☿ and ♂ .	8°	☿☌♂		♀ and ♄ .	44°	♀∠♄

♀ and ♅	.	47°	♀ ∠ ♅		2 and ♄	.	149°	2 ⊼ ♄
♀ and ♆	.	169°	No aspect		2 and ♅	.	58°	2 ⚹ ♅
♂ and 2	.	124°	♂ △ 2		2 and ♆	.	86°	2 □ ♆
♂ and ♄	.	25°	No aspect		♄ and ♅	.	91°	♄ □ ♅
♂ and ♅	.	66°	♂ ⚹ ♅		♄ and ♆	.	125°	♄ △ ♆
♂ and ♆	.	150°	♂ ⊼ ♆		♅ and ♆	.	144°	No aspect

This completes all the ordinary aspects, and only the parallels, if any, remain to be noted. Look down the list of declinations and note any two planets having the same declination within one degree, either both North, both South, or one North and the other South. This gives us ⊙ P ♀, ☿ P ♂, and ♂ P 2.

Having calculated all the aspects as above, tabulate them under the map.

The process of calculating aspects may appear to be a tedious one, but with practice it becomes extremely easy, and one is able to estimate the aspects at a glance. The following hints will be found of service :—

1. Two planets in or near the same degree of different signs are in aspect.

2. Add to, or subtract from, a planet's longitude 15°. Any other planets in or near the resulting degree *may* be in aspect.

3. Signs of the same Quadruplicity are in square or opposition to each other.

4. Signs of the same Triplicity are in trine to each other.

Numerous ingenious mechanical devices known as Aspectarians, and mostly emanating from America, are sold for the purpose of automatically calculating aspects. The beginner should strenuously resist the temptation to purchase one. They may save time and trouble at the moment, but they prevent one from visualising the aspects quickly, and are therefore a hindrance in the long run.

PART II
PLANETS, SIGNS, AND HOUSES.

INTRODUCTORY REMARKS

The following chapters describe briefly the persons and things ruled by each of the planets and signs, and the general effect of planets in signs, houses, and aspect. They were included here in deference to the opinion of certain elementary students, and only after considerable hesitation. That such information as is here contained is of use to the beginner is unquestionable, but the grave danger attaching to it is that it is apt to destroy the personal judgment. It is of the very utmost importance for the student to realise that these positions are necessarily described in general terms, and must not be taken as definite and unalterable. It is quite impossible to take into account even a tithe of all the variations that arise in practice, and the details here given should be regarded merely as hints. On no account should they be included as they stand in a delineation. The best use that can be made of them is to take each position, read over the description of its effect, and then try to puzzle out why such an effect should follow. This is excellent practice in developing the judgment. When the underlying idea has been grasped an even better exercise is to attempt to write a description of the probable effect of any position before reading it up. Then try to think out variations. Thus, Saturn in the 7th house is bad for marriage. Why? Because Saturn causes coldness, selfishness, and isolation, etc. Now try and think out the effects produced by Saturn in various signs in the 7th. Saturn in Leo in the 7th would be likely to import the question of children (Leo is 5th sign corresponding to 5th house) into the matter. Probably one of the partners would desire a childless marriage. If Saturn were in Taurus instead, the friction would arise over money or property. Practice along these lines will develop the judgment rapidly, and that is the object the student should set before himself to be attained at all costs. Success in astrology depends entirely upon *judgment* and nothing else. It is far better to write an independent delineation of only a few lines than to copy dozens of pages from books. The former encourages the judgment and increases its power every time, while the latter simply strangles it, and, moreover, furnishes a delineation like a ready-made suit of clothes which fits where it touches.

The following descriptions include the personal appearance given when the planets and signs are rising, and the character given when they are rising or ruling the horoscope. These may also be taken as personal descriptions of the wife, friends, and others according to the houses in which they fall and the persons they signify in the particular map. The occupations are little more than suggestions, and the diseases are those to which the person is subject provided the planet or sign is afflicted.

In all cases aspects will modify the general remarks. A bad position will be improved by good aspects, and vice versa. A position such as Jupiter in the 7th house, which normally shows a happy marriage, will produce an unhappy one if it is seriously afflicted. In fact none of the descriptions should be used without an eye upon the horoscope to see how it is supported or contradicted.

CHAPTER X

THE SUN

Appearance.—Full stature, round face, large head, large bones, fresh complexion, light and thin hair, blue or grey eyes.

Character.—Proud, dignified, honourable, generous, noble, ambitious.

Body.—Heart vitality, back, right eye of a man and left eye of a woman.

Diseases.—Debility, fevers, sunstroke, heart disease.

Occupations.—Jewellers, goldsmiths, managers and those in authority, government workers.

Persons.—Kings, noblemen, superiors, dignitaries, the father or husband.

THE MOON

Appearance.—Short, plump, broad face and chest, brown hair, pale complexion, grey and soft eyes.

Character.—Changeable, inconstant, capricious, receptive, sentimental, imaginative, good-humoured, fond of travel and novelty, modest, timid.

Body.—Stomach, breasts, sympathetic system, glandular tissues, left eye of a man and right eye of a woman.

Diseases.—Functional disorders, chills, colds, weakness, swellings, dropsy.

Occupations.—Sailor, traveller, caterer, servant, fisherman, advertiser, all whose work deals with liquids.

Persons.—The public, women generally, and especially the mother or wife.

65

MERCURY

Appearance.—Tall, thin, long limbs, dark hair and eyes, olive complexion.

Character.—Clever, wary, subtle, cunning, quick, active, alert, talkative, restless.

Body.—Nerves, lungs, brain, bowels, hands, arms, tongue, hair.

Diseases.—Nerve disorders, lung diseases, worry, insomnia, food irregularities.

Occupations.—Writer, teacher, editor, clerk, secretary, bookseller, postman.

Persons.—Brothers, male cousins, neighbours, young men.

VENUS

Appearance.—Plump, short, round cheeks, smiling face, light-brown and smooth hair, blue or brown eyes, clear complexion.

Character.—Artistic, pleasant, sociable, gentle, refined, bright, affectionate manner.

Body.—Chin, cheeks, throat, lips, Eustachian tubes, reins, ovaries, kidneys, internal generative system.

Diseases.—Venereal diseases, ailments of the throat and kidneys.

Occupations.—Poet, artist, confectioner, milliner, embroiderer, scent dealer, flower seller, linen draper.

Persons.—Sisters, female cousins, young women.

MARS

Appearance.—Medium height, strong, large bones, sharp hazel eyes, prominent brows, red, light, or black hair.

Character.—Brave, confident, assertive, easily angered, extravagant, passionate, energetic, destructive.

Body.—Forehead, nose, bile, gall, muscles and sinews, external generative system.

Diseases.—Fevers, infectious and inflammatory diseases, operations, effusions of blood, sharp and painful disorders.

Occupations.—Soldier, surgeon, dentist, chemist, photographer, metal worker, butcher.

Persons.—Men of below middle age.

JUPITER

Appearance.—Well-built, dignified, oval face,. high forehead, brown or chestnut hair, blue or brown eyes, fresh complexion.

Character.—Generous, prudent, jovial, kind, sympathetic, charitable, courtly, proud.

Body.—Thighs, feet, right ear, liver, blood, pleura.

Diseases.—Apoplexy, pleurisy, disorders of the blood and liver, ailments arising from excess.

Occupations.—Lawyer, physician, clergyman, banker, clothier, grocer, tobacconist.

Persons.—Uncles and aunts.

SATURN

Appearance.—Lean, thin, large nose and ears, dark or black hair, pale or sallow complexion, deep-set eyes.

Character.—Careful, cautious, jealous, miserly, severe, industrious, cold and reserved, just, unrelenting, suspicious.

Body.—Teeth, bones, joints, left ear, spleen.

Diseases.—Colds, chills, rheumatism, weakness, chronic and lingering diseases.

Occupations.—Miner, labourer, coal merchant, dealer in land and property, plumber, architect.

Persons.—Old people.

URANUS

Appearance.—Tall, spare, rugged look with strongly-marked features, dark hair and eyes, pale complexion.

Character.—Eccentric, erratic, inventive, independent, romantic, critical, fond of unusual things and subjects.

Body.—Nerves, part of brain and spinal cord.

Diseases.—Nervous breakdowns, paralysis, spasmodic and incurable diseases.

Occupations.—Electrician, inventor, aviator, antiquarian, astrologer, government official.

Persons.—Grandparents.

NEPTUNE

Appearance.—Medium height, soft, plump, thin face, nervous or strained and startled look, soft silky hair, dreamy eyes, clear complexion.

Character.—Æsthetic, artistic, musical, imitative, very emotional, dreamy, psychic and intuitive, self-indulgent.

Body.—Parts of brain.

Diseases.—Obscure and incurable diseases, ailments arising from self-indulgence through sex, drugs, etc.

Occupations.—Sailor, dealer in tea and coffee, tobacconist, violinist, spiritualistic medium.

CHAPTER XI

ARIES

Appearance.—Medium height or over, thin, long neck, bony face, high cheekbones, narrow chin, hair crisp or wiry and sandy or very dark, bushy eyebrows, grey or greyish-brown eyes.

Character.—Ambitious, courageous, reckless, energetic, enterprising, impulsive, combative, independent, clever.

Body.—Head, face, brain.

Diseases.—Diseases of head and face, neuralgia, dental ailments, fevers, affections of the eyes.

Occupations.—Soldier, explorer, writer, veterinary surgeon, groom, coachbuilder.

TAURUS

Appearance.—Short or medium height, squarely built, often stooping, short thick neck, full forehead, lips, and nostrils, heavy jaw, hair dark and often wavy, full dark eyes.

Character.—Obstinate, plodding, patient, persevering, strong-willed, jealous, resentful, slow to change, sometimes indolent, fond of ease, sensuous, loyal, fixed opinions.

Body.—Neck, throat, cerebellum, ears.

Diseases.—Diphtheria, quinsy, fistulas, apoplexy, diabetes, throat disorders.

Occupations.—Real estate dealer, house agent, wool merchant, builder, gardener, farmer, singer.

GEMINI

Appearance.—Tall, slender ; long arms, fingers, hands, and

69

legs ; long and straight or bird-like nose, hazel eyes, dark hair, pale or sanguine complexion.

Character.—Clever, versatile, dexterous, curious, subtle, flexible, mathematical and scientific, nervous, vacillating, irritable.

Body.—Arms, hands, shoulders, lungs, blood.

Diseases.—Nerve disorders, consumption, bronchitis, asthma.

Occupations.—Journalist, writer, teacher, musician, clerk, surveyor, mathematician.

CANCER

Appearance.—Medium height, inclined to stoutness, often top-heavy appearance, broad forehead, full face, full cheeks, double chin in middle life, short but sometimes prominent or peculiar nose, bad or rolling walk, grey or light-blue eyes, very dark or golden-brown hair, pale complexion.

Character.—Changeable, quiet, reserved, ambitious, imaginative, romantic, emotional, sensitive, capricious, adaptable, sympathetic, sentimental.

Body.—Breast, stomach, chest, digestive organs.

Diseases.—Gastric ailments, dropsy, liver disorders, cancer, rheumatism, dipsomania.

Occupations.—Sailor, publican, barmaid, caterer, wine merchant, servant, washerwoman, charwoman.

LEO

Appearance.—Tall, upright, broad, strongly-built, large bones, full round head, light and thin hair, grey or sherry-coloured eyes, florid complexion.

Character.—Faithful, frank, ambitious, proud, generous, artistic, lordly manner, fond of show, often ostentatious, very fond of children, idealistic.

Body.—Heart, back, spine.

Diseases.—Heart disorders, syncope, palpitation, etc., lumbago, meningitis.

Occupations. — Artist, actor, manager, organiser, butler, coachman, schoolmaster.

VIRGO

Appearance.—Medium height or over, full forehead, neat quiet appearance, moderately plump, straight nose, grey or blue eyes, dark hair inclined to be thin on top, dark complexion.

Character.—Methodical, cool, practical, very critical, precise, faddy over trifles, inquisitive, shy, modest, quiet, prone to worry.

Body.—Bowels, intestines, abdomen.

Diseases.—Constipation, bowel disorders, dysentery, diarrhœa, dyspepsia.

Occupations.—Secretary, accountant, teacher, clothes dealer, stationer.

LIBRA

Appearance.—Tall, well-made, slender but becoming stout in middle life, round face, long and straight nose, regular features, short fat hands and fingers, blue or brown eyes, smooth brown hair, complexion good but ruddy or pimpled in later life.

Character.—Genial, kind, just, very humane, idealistic, artistic, fickle, rather selfish and shallow, desire admiration, lazy, fond of pleasure and society.

Body.—Kidneys, skin.

Diseases.—Skin and kidney diseases, Bright's disease, eczema, nephritis, lumbago.

Occupations.—Bank clerk, designer, valuer, pawnbroker, draper, jeweller.

SCORPIO

Appearance.—Medium height, often thick-set or squarely built, face often fat but sometimes with aquiline features, prominent brows, dark and intense or sometimes beady eyes, thick and dark hair often curly.

Character.—Bold, confident, sarcastic, critical, strong willed, persevering, brusque, sensational, impressive manner, fiery temper, fond of secrets and mysteries.

Body.—Urino-genital system, nose, bladder, appendix.

Diseases.—Venereal diseases, piles, ruptures, fistulas, infectious diseases.

Occupations.—Soldier, sailor, chemist, photographer, surgeon, brewer, oil dealer.

SAGITTARIUS

Appearance.—Tall, slender, well-made but sometimes stooping, long or oval face, rounded forehead ; grey, blue, or brown eyes ; brown or chestnut hair thinning at the temples, good complexion.

Character.—Good-tempered but irritable, frank, honest, impetuous, good natured, optimistic, independent, clever, quick, shrewd guesser, fond of horses and sport.

Body.—Hips, thighs, arteries.

Diseases.—Rheumatism, gout, sciatica, lung and nerve disorders.

Occupations.—Lawyer, clergyman, physician, horse dealer, groom.

CAPRICORN

Appearance.—Medium height, thin, bony, prominent features, long nose, narrow chin, thin neck, dark eyes, dark thin hair, thin beard.

Character.—Reserved, capricious, very ambitious, quiet, suspicious, melancholy, just, conscientious, unrelenting and unforgiving, cautious and prudent, selfish, economical or mean.

Body.—Knees, bones, joints, teeth.

Diseases.—Rheumatism, colds, chills, eczema and skin diseases.

Occupations.—Government official, politician, diplomat, farmer, farrier.

AQUARIUS

Appearance.—Medium height or tall, well built, oval or longish face, brown or flaxen hair, blue eyes, good and clear complexion.

Character.—Idealistic, artistic, humane, timid, scientific, fond of human nature and humanitarian schemes, quiet, happy disposition, very friendly and popular.

Body.—Legs, ankles, blood and circulation.

Diseases.—Anæmia, nerve and blood disorders, cramp.

Occupations.—Scientist, aviator, electrician, designer, poet, painter, company promoter.

PISCES

Appearance.—Short, often stooping, fleshy, full watery blue or dark eyes, small and short limbs, plentiful dark hair, pale complexion.

Character.—Kind, very imaginative, romantic, talkative, versatile, secretive, changeable, often muddle-headed and clumsy, fond of sensationalism.

Body.—Feet and toes.

Diseases.—Gout, dropsy, colds, tumours, bowel disorders, infectious diseases.

Occupations.—Fishmonger, brewer, bootmaker, hospital or prison attendant, nurse, imaginative writer.

CHAPTER XII

SUN

⊙ *in* ♈. Strong, well made, light hair, large eyes. Courageous, noble, energetic, wilful, excitable, independent. Strong constitution. Insomnia, and diseases of head and eyes.

⊙ *in* ♉. Short, thick-set, brown hair, grey eyes, broad face and mouth, large nose. Proud, conceited, amorous, obstinate, warm-hearted, autocratic. Apoplexy, syncope, diabetes, fits, convulsions.

⊙ *in* ♊. Tall, well-made, brown hair, grey eyes. Affable, courteous, mild tempered, versatile, ambitious, refined, studious. Consumption, lung and blood disorders.

⊙ *in* ♋. Short, brown hair, grey eyes, pale complexion, often deformed face. Indolent, amorous, ease-loving, easy-going, fond of home and mother, untrustworthy. Digestive disorders, tumours, rheumatism.

⊙ *in* ♌. Strong, well-built, full face, large prominent eyes, light or sandy hair. Just, honourable, proud, ambitious, dignified, generous, sociable, kind-hearted. Heart disease, spinal ailments.

⊙ *in* ♍. Medium height, slender, well proportioned, dark brown hair, grey eyes. Ingenious, scientific, modest, industrious, lacks self-confidence, rather melancholy. Constipation, bowel disorders, lung and nerve weakness.

⊙ *in* ♎. Tall, slender, oval face, full eyes, light hair, ruddy or pimply complexion. Extravagant, generous, sociable, romantic, kind, just, hopeful, artistic. Kidney diseases; skin, head, and stomach disorders.

74

⊙ *in* ♏. Squarely built, full and broad face, brown hair, dark complexion. Ambitious, overbearing, proud, unbending, passionate, quarrelsome, obstinate. Diseases of throat, heart, and urino-genital system.

⊙ *in* ♐. Tall, well-built, oval face, light brown hair, olive complexion. Generous, restless, proud, judicial, good-natured, enthusiastic, sincere. Disorders of blood, lungs, and nerves. Accidents.

⊙ *in* ♑. Medium height, thin, oval face, brown hair, unhealthy complexion. Just, ambitious, subtle, reserved, thoughtful, conventional. Rheumatism, constipation, melancholy, weak digestion and bowels.

⊙ *in* ♒. Medium height, well made, stout, round full face, brown hair, clear complexion. Vain, proud, ostentatious, idealistic, democratic, humane, sociable. Disorders of heart, eyes, and nerves ; defective circulation.

⊙ *in* ♓. Short, stout, round full face, grey eyes, light brown hair, pale complexion. Changeable, restless, extravagant, intemperate, easily led, hospitable. Consumption, blood and digestive disorders.

MOON

☽ *in* ♈. Medium height, plump, round face, grey eyes, light brown hair, good complexion. Rash, ambitious, irritable, enthusiastic, aggressive. Insomnia, convulsions, diseases of head and eyes.

☽ *in* ♉. Short, stout, grey eyes, brown hair, pale complexion. Kind, obliging, amorous, quiet, persistent, conservative. Throat disorders, quinsy, croup, tonsilitis, goitre.

☽ *in* ♊. Tall, upright, well-made, brown hair, good complexion. Ingenious, talkative, subtle, crafty, active, dexterous, fond of reading and novelties. Bronchial and pulmonary diseases.

75

$\mathcal{D}$ *in* ♋. Medium height, stout, round full face, brown hair, pale complexion. Changeable, peaceable, fond of ease, attached to home, emotional, sensitive. Dropsy; breast, stomach and digestive disorders.

$\mathcal{D}$ *in* ♌. Tall, strong, large bones, full face, large prominent eyes, light brown hair, sanguine complexion. Ambitious, persevering, dignified, artistic, generous, warm-hearted, susceptible. Blood and heart disorders, scrofula, convulsions.

$\mathcal{D}$ *in* ♍. Tall, oval face, dark brown hair, pale complexion. Reserved, covetous, melancholy, ingenious, quiet, analytical, irresolute, unpretentious. Bowel and intestinal disorders, eczema.

$\mathcal{D}$ *in* ♎. Tall, well made, handsome, light brown hair, pink and white complexion. Pleasant, sociable, popular, artistic, affectionate manner. Kidney, blood, and stomach disorders.

$\mathcal{D}$ *in* ♏. Short, thick-set, ill-made, brown or black hair, bad complexion. Malicious, abrupt, revengeful, selfish, determined, energetic, intemperate. Dropsy, tumours, urino-genital diseases.

$\mathcal{D}$ *in* ♐. Tall, well-built, oval face, grey eyes, brown or chestnut hair, sanguine or bronzed complexion. Generous, hasty, restless, kind, energetic, honourable, intuitive. Good vitality. Diseases of nerves, blood, and lungs ; weakness of hips and thighs, sciatica.

$\mathcal{D}$ *in* ♑. Short, thin, weak, dark straight hair, small features, bad complexion. Dull, mean, cold, selfish, calculating, covetous, fond of show. Poor vitality. Long illnesses, gout, rheumatism, skin diseases.

$\mathcal{D}$ *in* ♒. Medium height, well-made, stoutish, brown hair, clear sanguine complexion. Affable, courteous, ingenious, inventive, sociable, humanitarian. Blood disorders, anæmia, hysteria, debility.

☽ *in* ♓. Short, stout, round or bloated face, sleepy eyes, light brown hair, pale complexion. Fond of ease, self-indulgent, dreamy, inconstant, intemperate, easily discouraged, lack humour or common sense. Infectious diseases, dropsy, disorders of the feet.

MERCURY

☿ *in* ♈. Medium height, spare, thin, oval face, long neck, light brown hair, bad complexion. Ambitious, restless, exaggerative, quick, tricky, clever, hasty, quarrelsome. Headaches, neuralgia, insomnia.

☿ *in* ♉. Medium height, stout, thick-set, grey or hazel eyes, dark thick hair, swarthy complexion. Improvident, practical, stubborn, ease-loving, sociable, fond of money. Nervous throat troubles, hoarseness, convulsions.

☿ *in* ♊. Tall, upright, well-made, hazel eyes, dark brown hair, long limbs. Clever, shrewd, scientific, linguistic ability, witty, argumentative, inquisitive, mentally changeable. Bronchial and lung disorders.

☿ *in* ♋. Short, thin face, sharp features, small grey eyes, dark hair, bad complexion. Fickle, changeable, tactful, discreet, mean, grasping. Digestive troubles, colic, flatulence.

☿ *in* ♌. Tall, thin, large build, round face, broad nose, full eyes, light brown hair, swarthy complexion. Bombastic, proud, hasty, ambitious, contentious, fond of pleasure. Heart or bowel weakness, palpitation, fainting fits.

☿ *in* ♍. Tall, slender, long face, small dark eyes, dark hair. Subtle, scientific, critical, ingenious, sceptical, practical, good memory. Bowel and intestinal disorders.

☿ *in* ♎. Tall, well-made, full build, grey eyes, smooth light brown hair, sanguine complexion. Pleasant, ingenious, good talker, refined, broad mind, artistic. Kidney and urinary disorders.

77

☿ *in* ♏. Short, broad, dark eyes, dark curly hair, swarthy complexion. Critical, suspicious, ingenious, self-seeker, obstinate, sarcastic, uncertain temper. Urino-genital disorders, neuralgia.

☿ *in* ♐. Tall, well-made, large bones, oval face, large nose, brown hair, ruddy complexion. Rash, hasty, rebellious, talkative, quick but superficial mind. Sciatica, nerve weakness.

☿ *in* ♑. Short, thin face, bow-legged or crippled, brown hair, dark complexion. Peevish, discontented, suspicious, critical, irritable, scientific. Gout, rheumatism, bowel disorders.

☿ *in* ♒. Medium height, stout, full face, dark hair, clear skin, clear complexion. Scientific, obliging, inventive, humane, refined, intuitive, fixed opinions. Hysteria, nervous debility.

☿ *in* ♓. Short, squat, pale sickly face, brown hair, hairy body. Fretful, repining, muddled, too receptive, imitative. Consumption, colic, disorders of the feet.

VENUS

♀ *in* ♈. Medium height, slender, blue eyes, fair hair, good complexion. Restless, idealistic, demonstrative, changeable, ardent. Eczema, skin diseases.

♀ in ♉. Medium height, plump, good looking, dark eyes, light brown hair, sanguine complexion. Kind, humane, voluptuous, obliging, strong feelings. Throat disorders.

♀ *in* ♊. Tall, slender ; brown, blue, or hazel eyes ; soft brown hair, clear fair complexion. Mild, kind, sympathetic, good humoured, just, charitable, liberal. Bad respiration.

♀ *in* ♋. Short, fleshy, round pale face, small blue, grey or greenish eyes, light hair. Gentle, indolent, fickle, economical, timid, inconstant. Digestive and breast troubles.

♀ *in* ♌. Tall, well made, round face, full eyes, light hair, freckled and fair skin. Generous, kind, passionate, proud, romantic, extravagant. Heart trouble, swooning, palpitation.

♀ *in* ♍. Tall, well made, oval face, dark hair, sanguine or dark complexion. Quick, active, musical, ingenious. Bowel irregularities, illness from wrong diet and indiscretion.

♀ *in* ♎. Tall, elegant, handsome, oval face, blue eyes, long and soft but not very plentiful brown hair, often freckled. Courteous, equable, kind, affectionate manner, popular. Kidney diseases, eczema, uræmia.

♀ *in* ♏. Short, stout, broad face, blue or grey eyes, dark hair. Self-indulgent, envious, jealous, seductive. Venereal diseases, disorders of womb and ovaries.

♀ *in* ♐. Tall, well-made, oval face, brown hair, clear complexion. Generous, good-natured, light hearted, fond of pleasure and sport. Lung troubles, gout.

♀ *in* ♑. Short, thin face, blue eyes, dark hair, pale and sickly complexion. Courteous, fickle, self-seeking, fond of pleasure, irresolute. Skin diseases, constipation.

♀ *in* ♒. Medium height, stout, brown or light hair, clear complexion. Quiet, affable, romantic, faithful, timid. Anæmia, hysteria, varicose veins.

♀ *in* ♓. Medium height, plump, round dimpled face, blue eyes, light brown hair, good complexion. Good-natured, just, affable, sympathetic, hospitable, impressionable. Tumours, chilblains, tender feet.

MARS

♂ *in* ♈. Medium height, well-set, large bones, grey eyes, light curling hair, swarthy complexion. Quarrelsome, positive, argumentative, courageous, proud. Brain fever, head and eye troubles.

♂ *in* ♉. Medium height, thick-set, broad face, wide mouth, grey eyes, dark coarse hair, ruddy complexion. Reserved, proud, conceited, bold, acquisitive, quarrelsome. Diphtheria, tonsilitis, stone, erysipelas.

♂ *in* ♊. Tall, strong, well-proportioned, grey eyes, brown hair, sanguine complexion. Rash, generous, ambitious, restless, ingenious, tricky. Bronchitis, pneumonia, inflammation of lungs.

♂ *in* ♋. Short, ill-made or deformed, grey eyes, scanty brown hair, sickly complexion. Peevish, revengeful, servile, ambitious, self-indulgent. Gastritis, typhoid and enteric fevers, puerperal fever.

♂ *in* ♌. Tall, large strong limbs, oval face, large grey eyes, light brown hair, sanguine or sunburnt complexion. Generous, noble, passionate, fearless, commanding, boastful. Malaria, pleurisy, aneurisms, heart trouble.

♂ *in* ♍. Medium height, well-made, round face, grey eyes, dark brown hair, dark complexion. Conceited, irritable, hasty, revengeful, shrewd, deceitful. Peritonitis, cholera, hernia, bowel inflammation.

♂ *in* ♎. Tall, oval face, light soft or wiry hair, sanguine complexion. Idealistic, courteous, quickly angered, conceited, fond of sport and the opposite sex. Inflammation of kidneys.

♂ *in* ♏. Medium height, stout, broad and plain face, black and curling hair, swarthy complexion. Passionate, acute, designing, revengeful, ambitious, ungrateful, quarrelsome. Piles, fistulas, venereal disease, stone, septic poisoning.

♂ *in* ♐. Tall, well-proportioned, oval face, quick eyes, brown hair, sanguine complexion. Hasty, generous, passionate, courageous, rebellious, loquacious. Sciatica, inflammation of lungs.

♂ *in* ♑. Short, lean, small head, thin face, lank black hair, sallow complexion. Ingenious, prudent, firm, witty, tactful, industrious. Rheumatic fever, jaundice, dysentery, skin diseases.

♂ *in* ♒. Medium height, rather stout, sandy hair, fair or clear complexion. Unruly, argumentative, nervous, clever, determined. Varicose veins, erysipelas, blood poisoning.

♂ *in* ♓. Short, fleshy, large eyes, light brown hair, bad complexion. Passionate, satirical, idle, deceitful, timid and bold alternately. Consumption, tumours.

JUPITER

♃ *in* ♈. Medium height, lean, oval face, quick eyes, high nose, light hair, ruddy or pimply complexion. Courteous, generous, noble, enthusiastic, judicial. Dizziness, swooning, congestion of the brain.

♃ *in* ♉. Medium height, stout, short thick neck, brown eyes, dark coarse hair, swarthy complexion. Firm, generous, peaceful, dignified, charitable, just. Gout, disorders from over-indulgence.

♃ *in* ♊. Tall, well-made, plump, full eyes, brown hair, sanguine complexion. Scientific, mild, affable, refined, literary, good-natured. Pleurisy, lung troubles, blood disorders.

♃ *in* ♋. Medium height, rather plump but disproportioned, oval face, brown eyes, dark-brown hair, sickly complexion. Courteous, conceited, kind, meddlesome or officious, talkative. Dropsy, indigestion, scurvy.

♃ *in* ♌. Tall, strong, full eyes, light-brown curling hair, sanguine complexion. Generous, noble, courageous, proud, loyal, ambitious. Pleurisy, apoplexy, fatty degeneration of the heart.

♃ *in* ♍. Tall, well-built, dark or black hair, ruddy complexion. Ambitious, boastful, prudent but rash, covetous, deceitful. Bowel and liver troubles, blood impurities.

♃ *in* ♎. Tall, slender, oval face, full eyes, light-brown hair, clear complexion but subject to pimples or rash. Generous, mild, obliging, considerate, just, fond of sport and recreation. Tumours, obstructions, and kidney troubles.

♃ *in* ♏. Medium height, stout, thick-set, full fleshy face, dark coarse hair, muddy complexion. Arrogant, ambitious, overbearing, industrious, covetous, selfish, crafty. Abscesses, dropsy, urino-genital disorders.

♃ *in* ♐. Tall, upright, oval face, brown eyes, brown or chestnut hair, ruddy complexion. Just, open, generous, kind, courteous, fond of sport and speculation. Gout, sciatica, leg and hip troubles.

♃ *in* ♑. Short, weak, small head, thin face, dark hair, sickly complexion. Peevish, discontented, autocratic, ingenious, severe. Eczema, skin troubles, bad circulation.

♃ *in* ♒. Medium height, stoutish, brown hair, clear complexion. Just, merciful, cheerful, humane, broad-minded, scientific. Lumbago, blood poisoning.

♃ *in* ♓. Medium height, fleshy, large eyes, light-brown hair, bad complexion. Good-hearted, generous, hospitable, sympathetic, charitable, friendly. Dropsy, tumours, poor blood conditions.

SATURN

♄ *in* ♈. Medium height, spare, large bones, small eyes, dark hair, ruddy complexion. Contentious, ambitious, touchy, industrious, boastful. Head, stomach and liver disorders.

♄ *in* ♉. Medium height ; heavy, lumpish and ill-made ; dark hair, dark complexion. Revengeful, dull, diplomatic, sullen, economical, sordid. Deafness, throat and voice troubles.

♄ *in* ♊. Tall, oval face, dark hair; dull swarthy complexion. Ingenious, subtle, scientific, self-seeking, unpolished. Consumption, pneumonia, bronchitis, rheumatism in arms and shoulders.

♄ *in* ♋. Shortish, lean, thin, languid eyes, dark hair, sickly complexion. Cunning, deceitful, repining, malicious, discontented, suicidal tendencies. Asthma, cancer, gastric and digestive disorders.

♄ *in* ♌. Medium height, large build, broad shoulders, sunk eyes, brown hair. Passionate, revengeful, generous, ambitious, cautious, conceited. Heart weakness, spinal diseases, gout, liver troubles.

♄ *in* ♍. Tall, spare, long head, plentiful dark hair, swarthy complexion. Scientific, melancholy, unforgiving, subtle, reserved, cautious. Constipation, bowel disorders and obstructions.

♄ *in* ♎. Tall, oval face, large nose and forehead, brown hair, clear complexion. Proud, argumentative, careful, opinionated, prodigal. Kidney, blood, and urinal disorders.

♄ *in* ♏. Short, thick-set, broad shoulders, dark eyes, thick dark hair. Malicious, jealous, avaricious, passionate, quarrelsome, violent. Gout, gravel, stone, urinal disorders.

♄ *in* ♐. Tall, lean, brown hair, ruddy complexion. Reserved, trustworthy, sensitive, loyal, proud. Consumption, bronchitis, sciatica, hip-joint disease.

♄ *in* ♑. Short, thin, stooping, long face, small eyes, dark hair and complexion. Suspicious, peevish, melancholy, avaricious, covetous, unforgiving, treacherous. Rheumatism, ague, skin diseases and bowel troubles.

83

♄ *in* ♒. Medium height, stoutish, large head and face, large grey eyes, brown hair, clear complexion. Prudent, scientific, industrious, thoughtful, observant. Cramp, anæmia, bad circulation, eye weakness.

♄ *in* ♓. Short, large head, full eyes, very dark hair, distorted teeth, pale complexion. Malicious, contentious, indecisive, fickle, lacks hope and courage. Consumption, rheumatism, colds, affections of the feet.

URANUS

♅ *in* ♈. Tall, thin, well-made, blue or grey eyes, light hair, ruddy complexion. Positive, masterful, abrupt, inventive, selfish, scientific. Inflammation of the brain, facial paralysis.

♅ *in* ♉. Short, thick-set, dark deep-set eyes, dark complexion. Determined, conceited, boastful, passionate, revengeful. Nervous throat disorders.

♅ *in* ♊. Tall, thin, grey eyes, light hair. Eccentric, scientific, inventive, inquisitive, generous. Asthma, cramp in arms and shoulders.

♅ *in* ♋. Short, stout, grey eyes, dark hair, pale complexion. Unreliable, erratic, capricious, changeable, conceited, restless, fanciful. Cramp of stomach, cancer.

♅ *in* ♌. Tall, large build, broad shoulders, light or sandy hair. Independent, resolute, generous, strong passions, proud. Heart stoppage.

♅ *in* ♍. Short, thin, small limbs, dark eyes and hair. Eccentric, studious, scientific, fond of novelties and curiosities, sensitive, retiring. Cramp in bowels, appendicitis.

♅ *in* ♎. Tall, strong, round face, light hair, sanguine complexion. Scientific, ambitious, easily angered, independent, romantic. Spasmodic lumbago.

♅ *in* ♏. Short, thick-set, dark eyes, dark hair, swarthy complexion. Malicious, deceitful, passionate, intense, secretive. Spasms of bladder, cancer of generative system.

♅ *in* ♐. Tall, upright, high forehead, grey or blue eyes, light hair, good complexion. Enthusiastic, scientific or philosophical, rebellious, turbulent. Sciatica.

♅ *in* ♑. Medium height, short thin neck, high forehead, steely eyes, dark hair. Proud, austere, conceited, ostentatious, self-opinionated, acquisitive. Cramp or deformity in knees.

♅ *in* ♒. Medium height, broad face, light-brown eyes, brown hair. Ingenious, scientific, independent, eccentric, impressionable. Hysteria, nervous disorders.

♅ *in* ♓. Short, stout, ill-made, dark eyes and hair, pale complexion. Dull, eccentric, cantankerous, fanciful, despondent, unnatural tastes. Cramp and sweating in feet.

NEPTUNE

♆ *in* ♈. Medium height, slight build, long neck, brown dreamy eyes, light hair, clear complexion. Imaginative, poetical, unscrupulous, craves notoriety, resourceful. Brain and eye troubles.

♆ *in* ♉. Medium height, thick-set. flexible neck, dull blue eyes, creamy complexion. Musical, æsthetic, sensuous, coarse, depraved tastes. Eye and throat troubles.

♆ *in* ♊. Tall, slender, large eyes, light or brown hair. Sensuous, irresponsible, musical, humorous, tortuous mind, mischievous. Consumption, neurasthenia.

♆ *in* ♋. Short, slight, fleshy, round face, small greenish eyes, light hair, pale complexion. Wayward, emotional, unreliable, parasitic, impressionable. Dipsomania, hypochondria.

85

Ψ *in* ♌. Tall, slight, full brilliant eyes, light sandy hair, ruddy complexion. Romantic, passionate, idealistic, generous, artistic. Peculiar heart weakness.

Ψ *in* ♍. Medium height, oval face, wistful hazel or brown eyes, abundant brown wavy hair, darkish complexion. Demure, mysterious, scheming, deceitful, sensitive, illicit pleasures. Consumption of bowels.

Ψ *in* ♎. Tall, elegant, large liquid eyes, abundant brown or light hair, ethereal appearance. Visionary, intuitional, poetical, artistic, weak morals. Dropsy.

Ψ *in* ♏. Short, stout, forbidding appearance, dark eyes, heavy brows, dark hair, swarthy complexion. Aloof, deep, subtle, proud, mysterious, sensual. Venereal diseases.

Ψ *in* ♐. Tall, oval face, large blue eyes, chestnut hair, fair complexion. Utopian ideas, mystical, resourceful, frothy, far-sighted, restless. Nervous diseases.

Ψ *in* ♑. Medium height, short neck, dark blue or bluey-grey eyes, smooth and fine brown hair, pale or dusky complexion. Idealistic, political, cunning, designing, selfish, self-indulgent. Skin diseases.

Ψ *in* ♒. Medium height, plump; large brown, hazel or blue eyes; abundant brown hair, fair complexion. Artistic, plausible, humanitarian, improvident, deceitful. Nervous diseases.

Ψ *in* ♓. Medium height, stoutish, round full face, deep dark eyes, dark hair, pale complexion. Quiet, humane, sensitive, poetic, inspirational, dissolute, lazy. Dropsy.

CHAPTER XIII

SUN

In 1st. Generous, dignified, proud, ambitious, confident, boastful, fond of display, independent. Honour and success. Good vitality. Few brothers.

In 2nd. Free expenditure. Extravagant. Money comes and goes easily. Gain through superiors or influential people, and through Government.

In 3rd. Firm, scientific and artistic, stickler for his religion. Fame by writing. Honours to relatives. Many short journeys unless in fixed sign. Business involves travel.

In 4th. Inconstant affections, occult interests, pride in house or property. Little chance of honour until late in life, but success and fortune at the end. Good for the father unless afflicted.

In 5th. Fond of pleasure, spends freely. Few or no children. Liable to heart illness. Success with places of amusement or instruction.

In 6th. Taste for hygiene and medicine. Bad for constitution, and illness according to the sign.

In 7th. Proud, honourable, lofty and generous marriage partner. Good for partnership. Honour through marriage. Success in litigation. Honourable or influential opponents.

In 8th. Extravagant marriage partner. Honour after marriage. Fame at or after death. Danger of death in middle life. If afflicted, violent death.

In 9th. Honourable, firm, just, religious, proud, ambitious,

87

artistic. Voyages, and success or dignities abroad. Clerical or legal honour.

In 10*th*. Honour and preferment, success, fortune, high position. Success under Government. High patronage. Honour in middle life. Rises above birth status.

In 11*th*. Loyal to friends. Firm and faithful friends. Helped or hindered by influential people. Successful ambitions.

In 12*th*. Difficulty in proper self-expression. Danger of imprisonment, exile, or life apart from relatives. Enemies among people of high position. Triumphs over enemies.

MOON

In 1*st*. Ambitious, fond of fame, curious, receptive, timid, imaginative, fond of change and novelty. Changeful life.

In 2*nd*. Changeful and unsettled fortunes, sometimes success and riches but loss and trouble if afflicted. Gain or loss by women, the public, or travel.

In 3*rd*. Capricious, unstable, scientific or occult interests. Gains publicity. Many short journeys. Help or hindrance from relatives.

In 4*th*. Often changes residence. Success in land work and farming. Uncertain position. Chance of inheritance. Popularity at end of life. Favours from women. Outlives wife. Lives near water.

In 5*th*. Fond of gambling, speculation, theatres, and pleasure, and success in these if well aspected. Many children, one becoming famous. Twins if in a mutable sign.

In 6*th*. Bad for health, especially to women. Much sickness in infancy. Many changes of servants. Makes good servant but bad master. If a servant himself, has many small things to attend to.

In 7th. Many journeys and changes. Success or the reverse in marriage and partnership. Fickle partner. Changeful relations with opposite sex. Unpopular. Public opposition. Enemies among women.

In 8th. Money by marriage, or unsettled fortunes after marriage. If afflicted, violent death. Death in public place or among strangers.

In 9th. Romantic, fanciful, curious, fond of novelties, bigoted in religion. Voyages and travel. Help from relatives by marriage.

In 10th. Desires public life. Changes in occupation, and unstable position. Benefit or the reverse from association with women. Deals in public commodities.

In 11th. Many acquaintances but few friends. Acquaintances among the public. Unreliable friends. Patronage of women. Several children if in watery sign.

In 12th. Hinders self-expression. Many secrets in the life. Enemies among women and the public. Danger of restraint or enforced retirement.

MERCURY

In 1st. Business ability, active and enquiring mind, restless, inquisitive. Many journeys. Literary interests.

In 2nd. Money by letters, writing, and other Mercurial activities. Loss by theft or trickery if afflicted.

In 3rd. Busy mind, scientific, mathematical ability, studious, inquisitive, changeable. Many short journeys. Crafty relatives.

In 4th. Inconstant affections, studious. Changes of residence for business purposes. Lives near buses, trams, libraries, etc. Inheritance by craft.

In 5th. Inconstant in love. Inclined to gambling or

speculation and worries through these. Bad for children, who may be deformed or mentally afflicted.

In 6th. Interested in medicine, hygiene, diet, etc. Danger of consumption and illness through worry or strain. Deceitful servants and employees. Loss by theft. Worries over servants, journeys, or health.

In 7th. Fomenter of quarrels. Many worries and vexations. Annoyance and competition in business. Troubles through litigation. Sharp-tongued marriage partner, domestic quarrels, and unsettled married life.

In 8th. Inconstant fortunes. Minor financial troubles after marriage, and worry over partner's money. In women's map, difficulty in obtaining money from the husband.

In 9th. Clever, busy mind, meddlesome, quick wit, scientific, literary. Inclines to travel. Legal worries.

In 10th. Talented. Literary and commercial success. Several occupations. Uncertain position. Success in trading and general agencies, or as secretary to influential person.

In 11th. Many acquaintances but few friends. Scientific friends. Worries through associates.

In 12th. Self-absorbed and narrow mind. Given to plotting and scheming. Many small enmities. Crafty enemies. Liable to scandal and slander.

VENUS

In 1st. Artistic, attractive, affectionate manner, fond of pleasure and personal adornment. Social interests and success.

In 2nd. Money comes easily. Gain through women, art, and drama. Expenditure on ornament, pleasure, or women.

In 3rd. Artistic, pleasant mind. Help from relatives and neighbours. Pleasant journeys.

In 4th. Fond of home and attached to the mother. Inheritance, and gain through parents. Happy and peaceful end of life.

In 5th. Given to pleasure. Large family. Success in love affairs and society. Gain by art, children, theatres, pleasure, and speculation. Artistic and affectionate children.

In 6th. Obliging servants. Good health. Love of clothes and adornment. Careful in diet. Health improves or suffers after marriage.

In 7th. Early and happy marriage or attachment. Gain through adversaries. Peaceful end to quarrels.

In 8th. Gain by marriage and legacy. Wife fond of ornament and pleasure. Financial success after marriage.

In 9th. Gentle, cultured, religious, cheerful, musical, and artistic. Pleasant journeys. Benefit through relatives by marriage. Honours received either with or without cause.

In 10th. Success, honour, fortune. Peaceful and secure position. Gain by women. Success in love affairs. Marries above his station.

In 11th. Many friends among women. Fond of society. Happiness through friends. Favours from women.

In 12th. Peaceful seclusion. Fond of large animals. Unfortunate marriage or mésalliance. Danger of enmity from women owing to secret love affairs.

MARS

In 1st. Strong, courageous, confident, consequential, assertive, passionate, independent, reckless. Often mark or scar on head or face.

In 2nd. Lavish, careless, and improvident. Loss by rashness. Good earning powers.

In 3rd. Stubborn, headstrong. Quarrels and loss through

letters. Loss by litigation. Disputes with relatives and neighbours. Fond of change. Danger of accidents by rail and on journeys.

In 4th. Troubles in old age. Bad for the father. Loss by fire or theft at residence. Quarrels with parents. Loss by speculation in buildings, property, and mines. Lives near railway.

In 5th. Fond of pleasure. Loss by gambling or speculation. Rash love affairs. Quarrels in home life. Children unruly and some die early. Danger in childbirth. Severe with children.

In 6th. Extravagant in food and dress. Feverish and inflammatory illnesses. Theft from servants. Strife in employment.

In 7th. Disputatious and quarrelsome. Excites opposition and strife. Subject to violence. Business enemies. Bad for partnership. Unfortunate marriage, with quarrels and separation or death of partner.

In 8th. Extravagant marriage partner. No money by marriage. Strife over wills and legacies. Loss by fire and theft. Quick or violent death.

In 9th. Headstrong, jealous, fanatical, atheistic, or bigoted. Fights for convictions. Loss in lawsuits. Danger in voyages and violence abroad. Loss by marriage relatives.

In 10th. Courageous, conceited, passionate, quarrelsome, desires conquest. Liable to slander. Success as soldier, otherwise danger of discredit.

In 11th. Friends among surgeons, soldiers, mechanics, etc. Quarrels with friends. Malicious friends cause injury and loss. Led into extravagance or dissipation by friends. Danger to wife in childbirth.

In 12th. Secret enemies. Loss by robbery. Danger from

large animals. Liable to imprisonment. Violence from enemies. Marriage partner suffers from inflammatory diseases.

JUPITER

In 1st. Dignified, generous, just, fortunate. Proud and hypocritical if afflicted. Good health. Social and business success.

In 2nd. Wealth and prosperity if well aspected ; otherwise great extravagance. Gain or loss by speculation.

In 3rd. Refined mind, optimistic. Pleasant short journeys. Help from relatives and neighbours.

In 4th. Happy and comfortable old age, but dies poor if afflicted. Father in good position. Gain by inheritance. Success in place and country of birth.

In 5th. Dutiful children who do well in the world. Gain by speculation if well aspected. Prospect of rich inheritance.

In 6th. Good health. Good servants. Many comforts. Chief illnesses through indulgence or excess.

In 7th. Good for law and partnership. Good for marriage unless afflicted. Faithful partner. Enemies become friends, or benefit arises out of strife.

In 8th. Money by marriage or legacy. Death peaceful or in peaceful surroundings and conditions.

In 9th. Religious, moral, prudent. Gain abroad. Advancement in the Church. Benefit by travel and through marriage relatives.

In 10th. Success, honour, esteem. High position. Public appointments. Rise in life. Gain through parents or superiors.

In 11th. Faithful friends and success through them. Ambitions realised. Association with people of noble birth. Good for children. Success at the time of the birth of a child.

In 12th. Few secret enemies, and those harmless. Success abroad, or in connection with large animals or institutions.

SATURN

In 1st. Industrious, economical, thoughtful, patient, shy, nervous, and if afflicted harsh, stubborn, and melancholy. Organising ability. Liable to bruises to the head.

In 2nd. Trouble, loss, and worry in money matters. Business losses and sometimes poverty. Very hard work with inadequate return. If well aspected, money by investment, from corporations, or money tied up.

In 3rd. Melancholy. Late mental development. Danger of loss in travel. Unpleasant journeys. Quarrels and loss by relatives and neighbours. Loss by writing, and trouble through publications and correspondence. Health suffers by travel.

In 4th. Early death of father. Tied to a locality detrimentally. Poverty at end of life. If well aspected, gain by land, property, and mines.

In 5th. Ungrateful children, or severe with children. Often denies or destroys offspring. Disappointment in love affairs. Danger of heart trouble or drowning.

In 6th. Fastidious tastes. Debility. Long and tedious illnesses, and illness through cold, want, or exposure. Tendency to fasting. Bad servants. Hard work if under others.

In 7th. Many open enemies. Loss by partnership and litigation. Cold, morose, reserved marriage partner. Death of partner. May marry widow or widower, or someone of differing age or station.

In 8th. No money by marriage. Trouble over, or loss of, legacies. Difficulties after marriage. Lingering death.

In 9th. Religious, thoughtful, studious, philosophical,

94

reserved, prudent. Danger and trouble abroad and in travel. Loss by marriage relatives.

In 10th. Trouble to mother or loss of parent in early life. Success and high position but ultimate fall and disgrace.

In 11th. Frustrated ambitions. Loss through false friends. Trouble to or from children.

In 12th. Secluded life. Injury through secret enemies. Liable to false accusation and imprisonment. Lingering illness of marriage partner.

URANUS

In 1st. Original, eccentric, inventive, abrupt, independent, stubborn. Unusual interests. Danger of falls and hurts by machinery. Estranged from parents and relatives.

In 2nd. Sudden gains and losses. Difficulty and perplexity in money matters. Many ups and downs. Money through Government or in unusual ways, and often earned at home.

In 3rd. Independent, scientific, and occult interests. Unpopular ideas. Many changes. Purchases curious books. Trouble through letters and journeys, and with relatives and neighbours.

In 4th. Estranged from parents. Trouble over inheritance and in old age. Many changes of residence. Sudden end.

In 5th. Inconstant in love affairs. Romantic attachments. Broken engagement. Domestic trouble. Strange sex ideas. Trouble through children, if any, but often denies or destroys them. Loss in speculation.

In 6th. Trouble and loss through inferiors. Obscure and nervous diseases. Health suffers through changes.

In 7th. Violent, cruel, or adulterous partner. Hasty and unhappy marriage followed by death or separation. Bad for law and partnership. Many open enemies and public strife. Great opposition in life, and perpetual quarrels with associates.

In 8th. Financial difficulties after marriage. Partner squanders money. Trouble over legacy. Sudden and extra-ordinary death, or death by nervous affliction, paralysis, or suicide.

In 9th. Independent. Unorthodox religious views. Fond of occultism, science, literature, or antiquarianism. Misfortune abroad or in travel. Loss or trouble through marriage relatives.

In 10th. Strong originality. Chequered career. Difficulties with employers. Scandal. Sudden changes in business. High position followed by fall. Estranged from relatives.

In 11th. Romantic love affairs. Impulsive and unfortunate attachments. Eccentric or occult friends, and loss through friends and acquaintances.

In 12th. Many secret enemies, and unexpected enmities. Loss by theft. Estrangement or exile. Imprisonment abroad or in strange places.

NEPTUNE

In 1st. Psychic, receptive, dreamy, inconstant, wandering, visionary. Sea life. Danger from plots and enemies. Liable to wasting disease.

In 2nd. Loss by fraud. Involved financial affairs. Gain through secret work. Money in peculiar or questionable ways.

In 3rd. Inventive, psychic, occult interests. Strange ideas. Adopts pseudonym or changes name. Fraud from relatives or neighbours. Afflicted relatives.

In 4th. Trouble to a parent. Family skeletons. Domestic troubles, and loss by domestic plots and over property. Secluded end, often in institution.

In 5*th*. Love troubles and illicit love affairs. Depraved tastes and peculiar sex ideas. Illegitimate children, and disappointment through children. Loss by speculation.

In 6*th*. Dislikes exertion. Peculiar tastes in food and clothing. Treacherous servants or employees. Liable to wasting disease.

In 7*th*. Treachery and loss by litigation. Peculiar marriage conditions. Crippled or afflicted marriage partner. Platonic or immoral union. Illicit attachments after marriage.

In 8*th*. Many troubles after marriage. Peculiar death in trance condition. Delays in culmination of ambitions. Inheritance divided, or wasted by litigation.

In 9th. Clairvoyant, psychic. Loss by fraud and the law. Difficulties abroad. Ocean voyages.

In 10*th*. Trouble to a parent. Strange career. Lack of application. Honour under assumed name. Too many lines of work. Dissatisfied with the profession.

In 11*th*. Seductive, unreliable, or treacherous friends. Secret love affairs. Illegitimate child. Loss by speculation.

In 12*th*. Despondent. Periods of poverty. Loss by fraud, plots, and deception. Many secret enemies and perils. Danger of confinement or imprisonment.

CHAPTER XIV

☉—☽

Good. Ambitious, loyal, popular. Favourable for health, general success, domestic life, and marriage. Help from superiors.

Bad. Domestic trouble, difficulties in the occupation and in dealing with the public. Bad for general health and affairs.

The Conjunction is a rather critical position depending upon the sign occupied and the other aspects it receives. It causes the health and mind to be easily upset, and makes the nature rather one-sided.

☉—☿

(Never more than 28° apart)

♂ *or* P. Good memory, studious, quick at learning and figures. Not always a good position, and may tend to cause superficiality and impair the intellect to some extent.

☉—♀

(Never more than 48° apart)

♂ *or Good.* Artistic, affectionate manner ; fond of society, friends, and pleasure ; popular. Favourable for money.

Bad. Only the semisquare can be formed. Fond of pleasure but liable to hindrances or excess. Affections too prodigal. Somewhat extravagant.

☉—♂

Good. Energetic, courageous, self-reliant, enterprising, generous. Strong body and vitality. Responsible position in army, public life, or ♂ occupation. Often brings legacy.

♂.or *Bad.* Rash, headstrong, quarrelsome, extravagant. Trouble to or from the father. Quarrels with superiors. Good vitality, but liable to accidents and fevers. Very bad for women, bringing trouble through marriage or a bad husband.

☉ — ♃

♂ or *Good.* Honest, optimistic, generous, charitable. Success, wealth, fame. Help from powerful friends. Good health. Favours professional occupations.

Bad. Wasteful, conceited, rash, extravagant, hypocritical. Loss of money. General bad luck. Danger of legal losses and trouble through travel, religion, or enmity.

☉—♄

Good. Steady, thoughtful, persevering, hard-working, ambitious. Favours responsible position or Government work. Help from elderly and influential people. Good for investment and gain through property.

♂ or *Bad.* Selfish, cold, unsympathetic. Generally unfortunate in life. Thwarted ambitions. Trouble to or from the father, and through superiors, elderly people, and the public. Very bad for health and vitality. Delays marriage in a woman's map.

☉—♅

Good. Inventive, original, ambitious, independent. Public work. Government or municipal occupation. Occult interests. Unexpected benefits. Romantic attachments in woman's map.

♂ or *Bad.* Stubborn, highly strung, perverse, eccentric. Loss in public affairs. Sudden catastrophes and reversals. Broken ties. Trouble to or from parents.

☉—♆

♂ or Good. Subtle, æsthetic, musical, psychic, fond of luxury. Benefit through watery occupations, speculation, and dealing with the public.

Bad. Unpractical, tricky, self-indulgent, immoral. Opposition in business; failure of projects; disfavour of superiors; loss by treachery.

☽—☿

♂ or Good. Strong, active, and quick mind; changeable, quick wit, good linguist. Good for travel, writing, study, and other ☿ activities.

Bad. Clever, independent, erratic and turbulent mind; given to gossip, lying, and backbiting. Danger of slander and adverse criticism. Trouble through writing and ☿ matters.

☽—♀

♂ or Good. Gentle, affectionate, artistic, tidy. Good for money, popularity, marriage, and artistic work. Help from women.

Bad. Slovenly, untidy, indolent; foolish, extravagant. Loss by women. Danger of scandal. Domestic and matrimonial troubles. Social unpopularity.

☽—♂

Good. Courageous, enterprising, practical, active, hardworking. Strong vitality. Gain by legacy, personal energy, and ♂ occupations.

♂ or Bad. Headstrong. unruly, rash, quick mind, quarrelsome. Liable to accidents and fevers. Unhappy marriage involving financial loss. Trouble to or from the mother.

☽—♃

♂ or Good. Honest, generous, sympathetic, hospitable. Favours wealth, success, and popularity. Good health. Happy domestic life. Gain by speculation.

Bad. Careless, hypocritical, extravagant. Loss by squandering, speculation, and dishonesty. Domestic troubles. Liable to gout, and stomach, liver, and blood disorders.

☽—♄

Good. Patient, persevering, thrifty, careful, steady. Fortunate for business advancement. Benefits from parents. Responsible position.

♂ or Bad. Ambitious, subtle, selfish, mean, suspicious, timid. Danger of poverty, business losses, and failure. Unfortunate marriage. Hard life. Poor health and digestion.

☽—♅

Good. Active mind, original, independent, occult interests. Frequent journeys. Attachments after marriage.

♂ or Bad. Eccentric, changeable, uncertain temper. Nerve strain. Matrimonial trouble and separation. Sudden and unexpected changes.

☽—♆

♂ or Good. Imaginative, emotional, dreamy, musical. Psychic power or interests. Benefit through the mother. Travel by water.

Bad. Self-indulgent, immoral, subtle, tricky or unpractical, tortuous mind. Loss from women. Scandal and slander. Secret enemies. Trouble late in life. Peculiar illnesses.

☿—♀

(Never more than 76° apart)

♂ or Good. Cheerful, sociable, artistic, refined, polished,

101

popular. Fond of young people. Benefits from relatives. May marry a relative.

Bad. Unimportant. Obstacles in social life, relations with interiors or relatives, and artistic activities.

☿—♂

Good. Quick active mind, shrewd, sarcastic, original, good arguer, mathematical ability, manual dexterity. Favours ♂ occupations. Legacy from a relative.

♂ or Bad. Same mental qualities, but exaggerative, quarrelsome, turbulent, very ambitious. Liable to mental strain and overwork. Loss by own or others' dishonesty. Trouble with relatives.

☿— ♃

♂ or Good. Tolerant, broad-minded, honest, generous, philosophical, good judgment. Favours general success. Professional occupation. Gain by literary work or relatives.

Bad. Good-natured, hasty, unreasonable, changeable. Poor judgment. Irreligious, sceptical, or blindly credulous. Loss by law. Trouble through travel or inferiors.

☿—♄

Good. Steady, methodical, grave, thoughtful, conscientious, logical. Responsible position. Good organising and executive powers.

♂ or Bad. Suspicious, critical, contentious, narrow, hard, malicious, easily depressed. Defective hearing or speech. May be dishonest. Separation from relatives. Unfaithful friends.

☿—♅

♂ or Good. Ingenious, intuitive, inventive, independent. Brilliant and original mind. Favours occult and scientific pursuits.

Bad. Original, eccentric, hypercritical, sarcastic. Liable to criticism and opposition. Trouble through writing and relatives. Liable to nervous breakdown.

☿—♆

♂ or Good. Intuitive, psychic, changeable, subtle, musical and artistic. Versatile mind. Mystical interests.

Bad. Unpractical, dreamy, bohemian, tricky. Psychic interests. Loss through treachery and slander. Liable to worry and suffer from vague fears.

♀—♂

Good. Demonstrative, generous, fond of pleasure and society. Benefits through opposite sex. Early marriage. Money through marriage and partnership.

Bad. Extravagant, careless, lax morality, too fond of pleasure, over-ardent. Loss by women and false friends. Trouble in love and marriage through death or separation.

The ♂ is variable, but usually causes indiscreet action.

♀—♃

♂ or Good. Sociable, refined, genial, chaste. Fond of beauty and dress or ornament. Generous. Favours success and popularity.

Bad. Insincere, flatterer, extravagant, indiscreet, proud. Lives beyond his means. Squanders on dress, ornament, or women.

♀—♄

Good. Steady, persevering. Faithful friendships and attachments. Late marriage or elderly partner. Gain through investment, marriage, or elderly people.

Bad. Selfish, restricted affections. Sorrow through love or marriage. Bereavement. May have depraved tastes. Loss by bad business or investments. Trouble through elderly people.

The ♂ is mixed, but usually more bad than good.

♀—♅

Good. Romantic, artistic, popular. Many friends. Early love affairs. Hasty marriage.

Bad. Jealous, romantic. Troubles in love and marriage. Loss by women. Irregular attachments. Delays or denies marriage in woman's map.

The ♂ is mixed, but usually more bad than good, especially in a woman's map.

♀—♆

Good. Emotional, romantic, susceptible, poetic and artistic. Many love affairs. Gain through art or friends.

Bad. Fickle. Unstable affections. Deception and disappointment in love. Danger of scandal. Loss by fraud and trickery.

The ♂ is of mixed effect.

♂— ♃

Good. Generous, enthusiastic, enterprising. Strong body and muscles. Apt to squander money or spend too freely. Given to championing friends or causes.

♂ *or Bad.* Over-optimistic, unduly enthusiastic, extreme opinions, very extravagant. Loss by gambling and dishonesty. Illness from fever or excess.

♂—♄

Good. Practical, severe, ambitious, determined, courageous. Gain from superiors and public work.

♂ *or Bad.* Hard, cruel, bad-tempered, malicious, rebellious. Liable to public discredit, scandal, imprisonment, or public death. Loss through superiors.

♂—♅

Good. Bold, headstrong, impulsive, powerful, proud, original, sarcastic. Favourable for science and engineering.

♂ *or Bad.* Violent and ungovernable temper, erratic, excitable, unbalanced, determined. Liable to accidents and sudden misfortunes and catastrophes.

♂—♆

Good. Strong emotions, generous, enthusiastic, conceited. Gain through medical work and the sea.

♂ *or Bad.* Self-indulgent, vicious, conceited, crafty, deceitful. Loss through women. Scandal. Danger from liquids and poison.

♃—♄

♂ *or Good.* Thoughtful, serious, steady, careful. Favours business advancement. Steady success. Gain by investment, property, and legacy.

Bad. Restricted ambitions. Bad luck. May be dishonest. Unsuccessful. Loss through public matters, property, investment, and by superiors, the law, and trustees. Seeks wealthy marriage.

♃—♅

♂ *or Good.* Original, religious, or philosophical interests. High position. Gain through legacy. May acquire wealth rapidly.

Bad. Unbusinesslike, headstrong, may be dishonest. Loss through the law, religion, and ♅ people and occupations.

♃—♆

♂ or Good. Sympathetic, devotional, hospitable, humane, conceited. Mystical religious feelings. Love of beauty. May have great financial success.

Bad. Emotional, conceited, hypocritical, impulsive, extravagant. Religious indifference or peculiar views. Loss by water and by fraud.

♄—♅

Good. Strong-willed, serious, thoughtful, altruistic. Prolongs life. Favours business success. Responsible position.

♂ or Bad. Stubborn, eccentric, strong-willed, malicious, may be indolent or criminally inclined. Weakens health. Loss through business, public affairs, and investment.

♄—♆

Good. Intuitive, self-controlled, subtle, acquisitive, thoughtful. Gain through psychic matters and liquids. Good for money and investment.

♂ or Bad. Cold, calculating, revengeful. Peculiar or depraved tastes. Liable to scandal and discredit. Loss by property and investment.

♅—♆

Good. Spiritual and occult interests. Inspirational. Strange life with many peculiar happenings.

♂ or Bad. Inspirational, unreliable, restless. Trouble and loss through occult matters. Strange and eventful life. Many misfortunes.

PART III
HOW TO JUDGE A HOROSCOPE

CHAPTER XV

THE PRINCIPLES OF JUDGMENT

The beginner usually sees in a horoscope a mass of disconnected influences of every kind, and is entirely at a loss to know how to proceed. Usually he reads the description of planets in signs and houses and gets very little further, chiefly because of the lack of any method. My object, therefore, is not so much to give a long list of rules as to indicate by way of example how to tackle the problem of judgment, leaving the student to fill in the smaller details after he has grasped the main principles.

Every planetary position in the horoscope can be read from various points of view. Thus all the planets and signs have some effect upon the native's character; all more or less affect his finances, his marriage, and every other department of his life. If we let the matter remain in this condition, however, the judgment of a horoscope would indeed resemble the solving of a jigsaw puzzle, but it is possible to simplify the proceedings considerably.

In every department of life one or two planets are of much more importance than the rest. These planets are called the *Significators*, and our task should therefore be first of all to find the significators of the matter with which we are concerned, and then judge chiefly from their positions and aspects. In fact the ability to judge a map accurately depends largely upon the power to select the significators correctly. In order to do this we have to consider two things. Firstly, what planets and signs are naturally connected with the matter under judgment; and secondly, to what house does it belong. Take marriage, for example. Venus as natural ruler of love

109

is obviously a general significator, and so is either the Sun or Moon, for the former rules the husband in a woman's horoscope, and the latter the wife in a man's. Then again the sign Libra, which corresponds normally to the 7th house, must also be important, and any planet in that sign must be considered. All these factors are quite general ones, and are true for every horoscope. They give the groundwork and colouring. The second consideration, namely the particular house concerned, gives the personal factor for that particular horoscope. In the case of marriage the 7th house is the one to be considered, and the final significator will be the planet in the 7th house or the ruler of that house. This gives the particular influences peculiar to that one map. Therefore we have general significators giving the tone, and a particular one pointing out the exact way in which the effects will be felt.

The planet ruling the sign on the ascendant is called the *Ruling Planet,* and is the particular significator of the native himself. The strength of this planet and the aspects to it indicate whether the native is strong or weak, free or hampered, and his general relations to his environment. It is of great importance in every enquiry.

Having found the significator of the matter concerned interpret all aspects to it as things and people affecting it. Suppose Jupiter were chief significator of money and afflicted by Saturn. We should judge that money matters would be hampered by poor conditions, depressing surroundings, ill-health, or whatever Saturn signified in that horoscope. In other words we should give Jupiter the chief consideration as significator of the matter enquired into, and interpret the action of Saturn in its relation to Jupiter, and not vice versa. On the other hand if Saturn were the significator we should judge that fits of generosity or extravagance would affect

110

the finances, because Jupiter is expansive in action, and its afflicting aspect would cause trouble and loss. This general judgment is then refined by taking into account the sign and

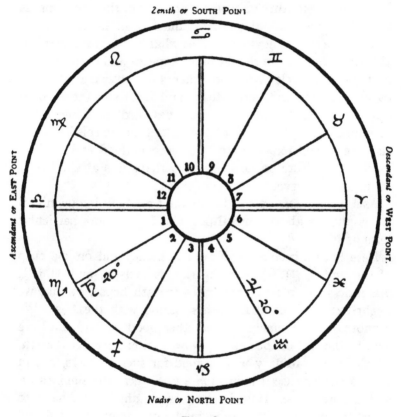

Fig. 8.

house occupied by the aspecting planet, and the houses it rules. Thus, suppose with Saturn as significator that Jupiter threw an adverse aspect from the 5th house. Then we should judge that the extravagance would arise from too much indulgence in pleasure, or from gambling, or other matters ruled by the 5th house. This would be modified by the sign containing Jupiter. A watery sign would incline more to self-indulgence, a fiery sign to gambling, a sign ruled by Venus to expenditure on women, and so on, thus enabling us to enlarge on the judgment obtained from house position alone. We should next look to see what houses Jupiter ruled. If it ruled the 3rd we should judge expense and extravagance over journeys, relatives, and other 3rd house matters, and by blending the influences, that gambling losses (5th) would come through the advice of relatives (3rd) or some other appropriate blending. If, at the same time, it ruled the 6th also, we should expect extravagance over food and clothes, much expenditure on health, and perhaps loss at the hands of unfaithful servants and employees.

As a general example of the method of obtaining definition let us put the above general positions into a more particular form as in Fig. 8.

Here Saturn is chief significator of money and on the cusp of the 2nd in ♏. The rising sign is artistic, and ♏ is a dramatic sign ; moreover, ♄ rules the 5th house, so that we might expect some financial association with theatres. We cannot at the moment say whether good or bad until we look to the rest of the chart. Now Jupiter occupies the 5th, which in the ordinary way is good for such matters, but in this particular case it is in square to Saturn, the significator, and denotes loss. How is the loss coming ? We have to blend the influence of ♃ in ♒ in the 5th ; and the 3rd and 6th houses and their signs, as these are ruled by ♃. Therefore we might say that a theatrical (5th) company (♒) financed by the native would cause great loss while on tour (3rd), possibly abroad (♐), owing to serious illness (6th) of the members (6th) possibly through eating fish (♓), or perhaps from malicious poisoning (♄ in ♏). This, however, is not the only way the influences would work. There would also be liability to great loss through the death (♏) of a child (5th) from consumption (6th house, mutable signs and ♒), which necessitated frequent journeys (3rd) to a hospital (♓). This is the method to be used, and it is one which needs considerable practice, but it is well worth the trouble involved, and the student will himself be amazed to find how accurately the most trifling details may be predicted.

As a word of advice to the beginner I would say—Do not be afraid to let yourself go in this way. You will make many mistakes to start with, but it is the only way to make your Astrology of practical use. There is too great a tendency nowadays to float about in a comfortable haze of so-called esotericism. The first need of Astrology is accuracy and definition, not pseudo-religious speculation, and it is only by concentrating on the practical and scientific side that we can really make Astrology of service, and obtain for it the recognition it deserves.

CHAPTER XVI

LIFE AND DEATH

The first question in regard to any horoscope is the length of life to be expected, and, in the case of a child, whether it is likely to be reared.

The chief factors for consideration are the ☉, ☽, and ascendant, which are all vital points. The signs in which they are placed are of importance, for some signs give considerable vitality, while others are weak. The relative value of the signs in this respect is as follows :—

Strong	♈ ♌ ♎ ♐
Moderately Strong	♉ ♊ ♍ ♏
Weak	♋ ♑ ♒ ♓

The strong signs give great vitality, and planets in them can survive considerable affliction. In ordinary cases they promise length of life. The moderately strong signs are inclined to be delicate and sensitive, especially in infancy, but give a moderate length of life. The weak signs are critical in infancy and their natives are difficult to rear, but they often strengthen as life advances. Under serious affliction, however, they promise only a short life.

Note the signs containing the ☉, ☽, and ascendant. If all are in strong signs and unafflicted a very long life may be predicted. If all are in weak signs and afflicted a very short life is shown; while mixed positions will give a longer or shorter life according to the severity of the afflictions. The ☉ rules the radical constitution, and the ☽ the functional and sympathetic system, so that in a general way afflictions to

the ☉ are more to be feared than to the ☽.   The worst
afflictions are from the malefics ♂, ♄, ♅, and ♆, and also
those from any planets that happen to occupy or rule the
8th, 6th, and 4th houses.   Benefic aspects to the ☉, ☽, and
cusp of the ascendant (which must be treated as if it were a
planet) from any planet tend to support life, and are most
beneficial if thrown by ♀, ♃, or ♂.

In the case of an infant particular attention must be paid
to planets close to the cusps of the angles.   A child will often
survive serious afflictions to the ☉ and ☽, and infant mortality
is usually shown rather by planets in square and opposition
across the angles, and afflicting the angles themselves, than by
ordinary afflicting aspects elsewhere in the map.

In judging of death note the aspects to the three vital
points.   When the afflictions are very severe, especially if in
or from ♈, ♉, ♌, ♏, ♐, or ♑, and the malefics are angular or
elevated while ♃ and ♀ afford little or no help, a violent
death may be predicted, but otherwise judge that death will
be natural and of the nature of the planets afflicting the vital
points, especially if they are in or ruling the 4th or 8th.   The
actual time of death can only be judged by a careful study
of directions.

General Example.   (Fig. 7, p. 51).

The ☉ is in ♒, a weak sign, afflicted by the ☽, ♄, and ♅,
and receives support only from ♀.   The ☽ is also in a weak
sign and afflicted by ♀, ♄, and ♅.   It receives the support of
♃ by semisextile, but ♃ is weak being in its detriment.   It
also has the sextile of ♆, but this is not vitalising.   The
ascendant is a weak sign, and is in sextile to ♅ and in trine
to ♃.   Therefore the afflictions and weak positions greatly
preponderate, and we should judge a very short life.   The

115

native would survive infancy, however, because the afflictions do not involve the angles.

The slight help to the ☽ and ascendant from ♃, and the conjunction of the ☉ and ♀ will prevent a violent death, but the affliction of both luminaries by ♅ indicates a sudden end after a long illness (Saturnian afflictions). Mercury ruling both 4th and 8th and in 12th indicates that the end of life will come in a hospital or institution. Anæmia, wasting diseases, and consumption are indicated by the afflictions to the ☉ and ♀, part ruler of 8th, in ♒, with ♃ in ♊ on the 4th cusp; Mercury, ruler of 4th and also part ruler of 8th, being afflicted by ♃ and also by ♂ in ♒.

CHAPTER XVII

PERSONAL APPEARANCE

The chief factors in describing the personal appearance are the rising sign and rising planet, if any. The appearance given by each sign and planet both singly and in combination will be found in earlier chapters, and there is little to add here. These form the basis and indicate the general type of body. Sometimes they are remarkably accurate as they stand, but modifications are often introduced by the sign position of the ruling planet, and by any close strong aspect to the rising degree. Thus ♂ closely aspecting the cusp of the ascendant often produces red hair, and ♄ black hair. Sometimes, if ♄ is two or three degrees away from the exact aspect the hair will turn black in as many years after birth as the aspect is degrees wide.

The position of the ruler is very important, particularly when ♋, and to a lesser extent one of the other watery signs, is on the ascendant. The effect is to introduce modifications in the appearance in accordance with the sign containing the ruler. Thus a normally tall sign rising may be considerably shortened if the ruler is in a short sign, and vice-versa. If ♋ is rising and the ☽ is in ♉, the body will tend to be short and squat, whereas with the ☽ in ♊ it would tend to be taller and thinner than the normal. As a rule the sign containing the ruling planet can be detected in the appearance, even if it is not very marked, and so can any sign which contains three or more planets.

The estimation of personal appearance is not at all easy, and the student is advised to study the published horoscopes of well-known people in relation to their photographs. The

117

following very mixed list gives the names of a few famous people born under the rising of the various signs.

Aries. King George V, Pres. Wilson, Savonarola, Carmen Sylva, Rudolph Valentino, Mrs. Annie Besant.

Taurus. Duchess of York, Pres. Hoover, Pierpont Morgan, Washington, Mary Queen of Scots.

Gemini. Queen Victoria, Duke of Gloucester, Pres. Ebert, Wagner, Tennyson, Dante.

Cancer. Ex-Kaiser Wilhelm II, Marshal Foch, Sir H. Rider Haggard, Sir J. M. Barrie, Rudyard Kipling, Huxley, Byron.

Leo. Prince George, Ramsay MacDonald, George III, Charles I, Bismarck, Betty Nuthall.

Virgo. Princess Mary, King Albert of Belgium, King Alfonso, Nicholas II, last Czar of Russia, James I, Pres. Coolidge, Earl Balfour, Gloria Swanson, Mozart, Chopin.

Libra. Duke of York, Lord Harewood, Emperor Franz Josef of Austria, Thomas Hardy, Gen. Bramwell Booth.

Scorpio. Queen Alexandra, Ex-King Manoel, Mussolini, Winston Churchill, Philip Snowden, John Burns, Edison, Dickens.

Sagittarius. King Edward VII, King Haakon of Norway, Abraham Lincoln, Lindbergh.

Capricorn. Princess Elizabeth of York, Pres. Hindenburg, Earl Haig, Gladstone.

Aquarius. Queen Mary, Prince of Wales, Lloyd George, Lord Baden-Powell, R. L. Stevenson, Ruskin, Jackie Coogan.

Pisces. Pres. Harding, Lord Rosebery, Earl Roberts, (?) H. G. Wells.

CHAPTER XVIII

The determination of character is one of the most important considerations in dealing with a nativity, for it is impossible to form a correct and balanced judgment unless the type of character is known and one is able to calculate the extent to which the native will react to any given influence. Every planet and aspect in the horoscope has an effect upon character, but to consider all these separate influences and make a satisfactory blend of them is a task rather beyond the beginner. The best way to treat the judgment of character is as follows :—

First of all count up the number of planets in each triplicity and quadruplicity. This indicates in a general way the basis of the character, according to which group in each division holds the majority of the planets. Cardinal signs give activity, ambition, love of fame, energy, a headstrong tendency, and restlessness. Fixed signs give obstinacy, will-power, patience, and resistance to change. Mutable signs give adaptability, nervousness, worry, indecision, and intellect. Fiery signs give energy, intellect, ardour, enthusiasm, and inspiration. Earthy signs give a practical, worldly, matter-of-fact and suspicious nature. Airy signs give an intellectual idealistic, and artistic nature. Watery signs give emotion, changeableness, and imagination.

Having settled the general type of character, study the rising sign and any planet rising in the same sign, even if it be above the ascendant and in the 12th house. This denotes the native's characteristics and outlook. We may look upon the horoscope as a house with many different rooms, and different things going on inside out of sight of the world.

The ascendant is the front door, and it is through this that the native must always appear. Every thought and act is finally coloured by the rising sign, and rising planet, if there is one. A horoscope with intense energy in the planetary positions and a weak ascendant will indicate weakness on the surface, and will spoil the inner strength; while conversely a strong ascendant that is unsupported by the rest of the horoscope will create a false first impression of strength.

Then look to the ruler of the rising sign, which is the chief significator of the native himself. The ruler weak by sign and house or retrograde denotes a hampering influence, and a lack of proper self-expression. Ezamine the ruler's aspects. Each of these will give the good or bad qualities of the aspecting planets according to the nature of the aspect.

Next take the Moon and its aspects. The Moon is the chief ruler of the personal characteristics and largely governs the habits, instincts, and to some extent the mentality. The planet in closest strong aspect with the Moon, especially if the aspect is separating, will colour the feelings and determine the general quality of the lunar influence.

The deeper aspirations and inner character are ruled by the Sun, which should have next consideration in the same way.

Finally, to determine the intellectual nature of the map study the planet Mercury and its aspects, as well as any planets in the 3rd and 9th houses. Remember that Mercury takes on the nature of the planet in closest strong aspect, especially if separating, and that the influence of this planet gives the prevailing colour to the mind. Such an aspect should, however, be within about 3 degrees, as otherwise Mercury tends to take on the nature of the planet ruling the sign it is in.

In the case of character many contradictory qualities will be indicated. These do not cancel out, though they are probably subject to mutual modification as life proceeds. The characteristics given by the stronger and more prominent planet will be the normal ones, and the others will be below the surface and appear only from time to time.

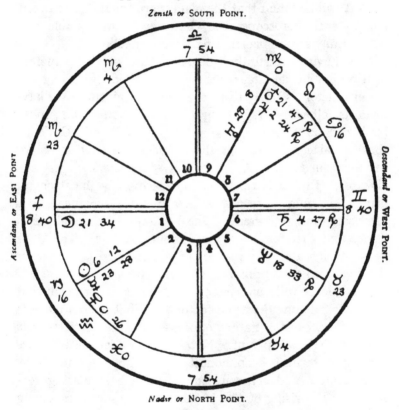

FIG. 9.

Example. Fig. 9.

There are 2 planets in cardinal signs, 4 in fixed, and 3 in mutable. This gives a preponderance of fixed planets, indicating patience, obstinacy, conservatism, pride, and organising power. Then there are 3 planets in fiery signs,

4 in earthy, 2 in airy, and none in watery. The earthy signs predominate, showing a practical nature, worldly, concrete, and suspicious. The blend of fixed-earth denotes materialism, obstinacy, self-esteem, and a methodical nature. In some cases it will be found that the planets are equally distributed, and in such horoscopes the character is an equable one, without any strong bias in a particular direction.

Now having noted the general nature of the planetary distribution in the signs, we have to decide which of the various factors is likely to be the most prominent. We have them as follows :—(1) ☽ rising in ♐ ; (2) ♃, ruler of ♐, in ♌ ; (3) ☽ in ♐ as before ; (4) ☉ in ♑ ; (5) ☿ in ♑. Omitting the mental significators for the moment, we have to choose between ☽ in ♐, ♃ in ♌, and ☉ in ♑ for the strongest significator. Jupiter is ruler, but not necessarily the strongest planet. In fact it is not so here, for it is succedent, in a fixed sign, and retrograde. The ☽, however, is angular and rising, and therefore in a very strong position. The ☉ is weak by sign and only just above the 2nd cusp, so we must clearly accord chief prominence to the ☽ in ♐.

It should be fully understood that this does not mean that we are to rule out the other factors. What it does mean is that influences of a nature opposite to those given by the ☽ in ♐ will be less apparent. Now let us consider this influence first. Sagittarius is open, honest, frank, impetuous, intuitive, good-natured, and generous, and usually has sporting tendencies. The rising of the ☽ adds to the restlessness, giving imagination, some sentimentality, and a love of change. The strongest lunar aspect is the trine to ♂. This increases the generosity as it is an outgoing and impulsive influence, and is thrown from ♌ and the 8th house, a house connected with money. This generosity and expenditure will show itself particularly in connection with domestic matters and friends, because ♂ rules the 4th and 11th houses. A fair amount of courage will be present, though more moral than physical, because ♌ and ♐ are fiery and mental signs and do not involve the physical body to any extent in this sense, while the strongly Saturnian nature of the map does not conduce to physical bravery. The parallel of the ☽ to ♃ is rather similar in nature in so far as it increases generosity and expenditure, and adds considerable optimism. Here, however, the influence is working through ♌, the sign corresponding to the 5th house, and as ♃ is also involved it will tend to increase the love of sport and speculation. Ruling the 1st and 3rd houses, ♃ also turns the extravagant tendencies towards self and relatives. The lunar parallel to ♄ is an influence of a quite opposite nature, causing apprehension and indecision as it is in a mutable sign, together with carefulness, caution, suspicion, and moodiness. Now how is this to be harmonised ? Obviously the ♃ ♂ tendencies are stronger, for these planets are elevated above ♄, and ♃ is ruler of the horoscope and of the sign containing the ☽. On the other hand, looking ahead, we see ☉ and ☿ in the Saturnian sign ♑. The latter influences are, as we have seen, lying further below the surface than those of ☽ in ♐, and therefore the Saturnian aspect will do the same. It will, in fact, act as a check upon the impulse of the positions already considered. The prevailing tendency will be generosity, but it will be checked at times, and there will be periods when ♄ will produce caution and worry owing to its position in the mental sign ♊. Extravagance and generosity will be impulsive (♂ ♃ in ♌), and time to think (♊) will bring misgivings. These will be chiefly concerned with money matters owing to Saturn's rulership over the 2nd house. Marriage will strengthen the caution, because ♄ is on the cusp of the 7th. The lunar square to ♅ will cause erratic tendencies or

123

an unusual outlook, with some abruptness at times ; while the weak semisextile to ☿ adds mental ability of a practical nature, since ☿ is in the practical sign ♑.

This is the general type of character with which we have to deal. The next thing is to take the other positions. Jupiter, the ruler, in ♌ has already been considered to some extent. Its aspects emphasise the above characteristics. Thus the opposition to ♀ is extravagant, and the sextiles to ♄ and ♅ introduce underlying carefulness, together with considerable ingenuity from ♅ in ♍, but again of a rather practical kind. The ♌ position introduces much pride and a liking for display and ostentation, which, however, is kept within bounds by ♄. Deeper in the character we have ☉ in ♑, an intensely ambitious and practical influence, giving subtlety, seriousness, reserve, some vindictiveness, and an unrelenting nature. We are therefore justified in saying that the native would be difficult to know, because the inner nature is very much at variance with the outer, and by no means so desirable. The solar aspects are all adverse, and do not tend to exhibit the best side of ♑. Mentally the influence of ♄ is also present, for ☿ takes over the nature of that planet, having no close aspect. Therefore we should judge the mind to be radically suspicious, practical, and concrete, and concerned more with business than with intellectual or artistic interests.

CHAPTER XIX

The occupation is denoted chiefly by the planet nearest to the ⊙, the planets in the 10th house or the ruler of that house, the majority positions of the planets, and the Ascendant. This is rather a lot to take into account, and indeed the determination of the occupation, especially nowadays when there are so many, is one of the most difficult branches of Astrology.

The best thing to do is to examine the general type of the horoscope to start with. The distribution of the planets in the triplicities and quadruplicities should be noted. If the majority are in Fiery signs there is a tendency to follow occupations involving fire and metals, and the native may be a soldier, surgeon, mechanic, engineer, etc. If Earthy signs hold the majority, the tendency is to manual occupations, farming, agriculture, mining, etc. ; if Airy, to intellectual or artistic work ; and if Watery, to work connected with fluids, such as sailor, chemist, painter, brewer, publican, etc., or to work bringing the native before the public, or to plebeian occupations. If the majority of planets are in Cardinal signs, the tendency will be towards managing and directing, political work, and an active or pioneering career ; if in Fixed signs, to plodding and routine work, production, manufacture, or Government or financial work ; if in Mutable signs to intellectual and clerical work, travelling, etc., and also to several changes of occupation, or to more than one occupation at the same time. The nature of the signs on the 10th and 1st should also be noted and included in the majority positions.

125

Having settled the general type of occupation to be expected, turn to the ☉, and note its sign and house position, and any planet that may happen to be near it. If ♂ be the nearest planet the work will partake of the nature of ♂, and will be active and probably connected with fire, tools, etc. Judge in this manner for the other planets. The house position of the ☉ often gives a further clue to the nature of the occupation according to the matters ruled by the house or the sign to which it normally corresponds. Thus the 3rd house, which corresponds to ♊, suggests work of a clerical or travelling nature ; the 6th house suggests service of some kind, or medical work, and so on. Finally note the planets in the 10th house or the ruler of that house. Aspects to these will indicate the fortunes of business.

The prominence and position attained is indicated by the strength of the planets. Many planets in angles or cardinal signs give fame or notoriety ; fixed signs and succedent houses give slower but more lasting fame ; while planets in mutable signs or cadent houses tend to obscurity. Many planets above the horizon or in the left-hand half of the map also tend to give prominence.

General Example. (Fig. 7, p. 51.)

There are 4 planets in Airy signs and 4 in Cardinal, while if we include the 1st and 10th cusps we have 5 Airy, 4 Cardinal, and 4 Fixed. Thus the general type of horoscope inclines to intellectual or artistic work through the Airy signs ; to management and directing or to originality through the Cardinal signs ; and to routine work through the Fixed signs ; The nearest planet to the ☉ is ♀, which inclines to artistic work, and its rulership over the 3rd house also suggests work of a mental rather than a physical nature. The sign ♐ is on the 10th, a fiery and inspirational sign, and its ruler, ♃, is in the mental and clerical sign ♊ on the cusp of the 4th house which rules buildings, houses, etc. We have to think of an occupation involving as many of these details as possible. Draughtmanship, designing, and architectural work immediately suggest themselves, and we must see how they fit in with the rest of the map. We have ♄, the ruler, in ♑, a sign of planning and organising and one which rules buildings, Mercury is also there, giving the right mental bias for work of this kind. Uranus in the 2nd house in sextile to the ruler of the 10th suggsts money from originality, and is quite in keeping with such occupations. The trine from the ruler to ♆ in ♍ is also beneficial, as it would increase the intuition, and help greatly with the detail work (♍). Thus we should finally judge architecture as a likely profession, with ability for designing. These, however, are not the only possible occupations by any means. Thus the Civil Service is indicated by the planets in ♒, a political or Government sign, and ♃ in ♊ for the clerical work involved. On a lower scale the native might become some kind of commission agent. In this matter it is essential to know the general environment and social standing of the native or his parents in order that we can confine our choice to occupations fitting the conditions.

CHAPTER XX

In judging the financial prospects of the native proceed as follows :—

1. Examine the ☽ and see whether it is strong and well aspected or the reverse. An afflicted ☽ is adverse for general conditions, and if seriously afflicted causes difficulty in obtaining money, and even poverty, especially if badly afflicted by Saturn. A good aspect between the ☉ and ☽ or benefic aspects to the ☽ from ♃ or ♀ conduce to comfortable circumstances or wealth according to the strength of the planets concerned.

2. Note whether ♃ and ♀ are strong. The stronger they are and the better aspects they receive, the better will be the fortunes.

3. As chief significator look to any planet in the 2nd house, or if that house be unoccupied, look to the ruler of the 2nd. The condition of this planet and the aspects it receives will indicate the financial fortunes and experiences in accordance with the general tone denoted by the ☽, ♃, and ♀. The planets throwing good aspects to the chief significator indicate the persons and things bringing money to the native, while the afflicting planets denote the sources of loss and expenditure. For the exact circumstances note the houses and signs occupied by such planets, and the houses they rule.

4. The 2nd house is concerned chiefly with the native's own money, and when judging of inheritance, legacy, and

128

money obtained by marriage look to the planets in, or the ruler of, the 8th house in exactly the same way. For the circumstances attending speculation take the 5th house and its ruler.

General Example. (Fig. 7, p. 51.)

The ☽ and ♀ are both badly afflicted. The former is in opposition to ♄, indicating general depression in financial affairs probably due in part to speculation or some other 5th house matter. The square from ♅ in the 2nd points to great and unexpected losses through headstrong action (♈), domestic affairs (♋), love affairs, and other 5th house activities. The aspects to ♃ are better, and the position of this planet on the cusp of the 4th denotes that the circumstances at the end of life will be more comfortable than in earlier years. But the weak sign position of ♃ denotes hindrances, and so does the square from ♆, so that we should expect the resources to be limited and probably in the form of an annuity, in the hands of trustees (7th), or so ordered that the native has difficulty in spending. Uranus in the 2nd has good aspects from ♂ and ♃, but is otherwise afflicted. This denotes ups and downs, with losses due to political and other Uranian influences, as well as to the matters signified by the afflicting planets. The sextiles from ♂ and ♃ promise windfalls, and some inheritance from a parent (♃ ruling 10th), but legacies will be lost or prove disappointing owing to the semisquare to ♀, part ruler of the 8th, though in one case something will be recovered through a lawsuit (☿, part ruler of 8th, ☌ ♂, ruler 9th ; and ♂ ⚹ ♅).

129

CHAPTER XXI

HEALTH

. The significators in this matter are :—

1. The ☉, ruling the vitality and constitution.

2. The ☽, ruling the functional disorders and sympathetic system. The ☽ is specially important in the horoscopes of women.

3. The Ascendant, ruling the body.

4. The 6th house and its occupants and ruler.

The strength by sign of each of these significators indicates its power of resisting disease and of recuperation. If strong and well aspected there will be little illness, but each affliction denotes a point of weakness, the exact nature of which depends upon the planets and signs concerned. Thus afflictions from ♂ indicate feverish and inflammatory diseases ; from ♄, ailments arising from colds and chills ; from ♀, diseases arising from pleasure ; from ♃, diseases due to excess, etc. ; and in addition there will be liability in each case to the special illnesses ruled by the planet and sign. The signs occupied by the ☉, ☽, and ascendant indicate sensitive parts of the body, and the same is true of the sign on the cusp of the 6th house, and that containing the ruler of the 6th. Finally any strong affliction in the horoscope may produce weakness in the parts of the body ruled by the signs concerned.

Accidents are caused by afflictions to the ☉ or ☽ from ♂, ♄, and ♅, especially when near the ascendant, and when any of these planets are in ♈, ♊, ♎, ♐, or ♑. Mars causes cuts, burns, scalds, and wounds ; Saturn, falls, sprains, dislocations, and bruises ; and Uranus, explosions, accidents from electricity, lightning, and machinery.

General Example. (Fig. 7, p. 51.)

The ☉ and ascendant are both in ♒, ruling the blood and circulation, and the ☉ is badly afflicted, denoting a weak constitution. The ☉ ∠ ♄ indicates poorness of blood, bad circulation, and liability to colds, rheumatism, and general debility ; ☉ ∠ ♅ is bad for the head and eyes, and indicates peculiar ailments, and illnesses through headstrong (♈) and erratic behaviour. The ☽ is in ♋, and also rules the 6th house. The sign ♋ affects the stomach and digestive organs, and the afflictions to the ☽ here will disturb these parts of the body. The number and severity of the afflictions indicates much illness throughout life. The opposition of ♄ will greatly weaken the health, especially as it affects both luminaries, and bring long and tedious illnesses, rheumatism, chronic gastric trouble, and danger of cancer. Being ruler of the 12th it shows hospital treatment. The affliction from ♀ indicates that indiscretion in diet will disturb the digestion (♋) and the blood (♒) ; and as ♀ rules the 3rd house the health will be disturbed by journeys. Kidney trouble is also threatened by this aspect, and by the numerous afflictions in cardinal signs.

Accidents are indicated by the rising ♂, and also by ♄ and ♅ in ♑ and ♈, afflicting both luminaries. The position of ♄ in ♑ denotes falls affecting the knees, and by its semisquare to the ☉ in ♒, the ankles also. Uranus afflicting from ♈ threatens sudden accidents to the head.

131

CHAPTER XXII

ASSOCIATES

The people, other than relatives, with whom the native is brought into contact are represented in the horoscope by the following houses :—

Friends—11th.

Secret enemies—12th.

Open enemies, opponents, and also business partners—7th.

Neighbours—3rd.

Employers and superiors—10th.

Employees and servants—6th.

The planets in these houses, or the rulers if they are unoccupied, taken in connection with the signs in which they are placed, will describe the personal appearance and character of the persons signified, while the condition of the planets by strength and aspect will denote the result.

To determine the result of association between the native and any particular person, the two horoscopes should be compared. This is done by noting how the planets in each horoscope fall in the houses of the other, and also the nature of the aspects thrown by the planets from one horoscope to the other. Thus if the benefics in one chart fall in the 10th house of the other, the person whose 10th house is affected will gain professionally from the other person. If they fall in the 2nd there will be financial gain ; in the 7th, gain by partnership or marriage, and so on. Again, if ♃ in one map falls on the ⊙ in the other, or favourably aspects it, the person

132

whose ☉ is affected will gain through the other along the lines indicated by the house and sign position involved. Similarly, adverse aspects will produce trouble and loss. In the case of marriage the best sign is a good aspect from the man's ☽ to the woman's ☉. Aspects between ♀ and ♂ in the two maps increase the sex attraction, but if adverse may cause difficulty in controlling the passions. The worst aspects for marriage, and indeed for any association, are afflictions among ♂, ♄, and ♅ across the maps.

General Example. (Fig. 7, p. 51.)

Saturn occupies the 11th house, indicating elderly friends, associates in Government positions, and friends of the type described by ♄ in ♑. The aspects to ♄ clearly indicate loss and trouble by friendship. Thus the opposition to the ☽ will cause loss by 5th house matters, and also illness through the influence of friends, the latter because of the Moon's rulership over the 6th house. Opposition will arise between the native's friends and his employees (6th). Similarly the other aspects show other sources of trouble or benefit.

Mercury in the 12th house indicates malicious secret enemies who will cause trouble through slander, and will affect the professional career (☿□♃, ruler of 10th). A death and a legacy will provoke enmity, since ☿ rules the 8th and afflicts ♃ ruling 2nd. The same planet being ruler of both the 12th and 1st houses indicates that the native will be his own enemy to some extent.

Other associates may be judged in a similar manner, and the particular details obtained by a consideration of the houses ruled by the aspecting planets.

CHAPTER XXIII

MARRIAGE AND CHILDREN

Love affairs are shown by planets in, or the ruler of, the
5th house ; and marriage, or union whether legal or otherwise,
by the occupants or ruler of the 7th.   The general significators
are the ☽ and ♀ in a man's horoscope, and the ☉, ♀, and ♂
in a woman's together with the planet in, or ruler of, the 7th.
Marriage will take place if the significators are in favourable
signs, especially if in a watery sign ; if a watery sign is on
the 7th cusp ; if ♀ aspects ♂ ; and if there are no afflictions
to the significators from ♄ or ♅.   The weaker and more
afflicted the significators, the less chance there is of marriage.
Afflictions from ♄ tend to cause delay, but sometimes denote
marriage to an elderly partner or one of low birth.   Afflictions
from ♅ are particularly bad in a woman's map ; they usually
deny marriage, but at times lead to seduction.   The significators in mutable signs or aspecting planets in these signs
indicate several marriages.   The wife or husband is described by the planet in the 7th, and nearest the cusp if there
are several ; or by the ruler of the 7th and the sign containing it if that house is empty.   The circumstances of
marriage are often indicated by the planet with which the ☽
in a man's map, or the ☉ in a woman's, first forms an
aspect after birth, and if the aspect is within orbs at birth
it partly describes the partner.   Thus application to △ ♂
would indicate an independent, capable, and energetic partner,
whereas if it were to □ ♂ it would denote one of a headstrong, wilful, quarrelsome and domineering type.

134

MARRIAGE AND CHILDREN

A second wife or husband is usually represented by the 9th house and its ruler; a third wife by the 11th, and so on; but sometimes the second partner is indicated by the planet ruling the sign containing the ruler of the 7th.

The time of marriage is estimated by considering the relative strength of the signs. If the significator is unafflicted and in watery signs an early marriage is indicated. The same is the case when the ☽ is passing from New to Full or is between the 1st and 10th, or 7th and 4th cusps. The opposite positions delay marriage, and so also do afflictions to the significators. The success or otherwise of the marriage is indicated by the aspects to the planets in or ruling the 7th. The length of married life is shown by the number of degrees between the significator and the next strong affliction it meets, counting each degree as one year.

Children are ruled by the 5th house. If there is a watery sign on the 5th, or the ruler is in a watery sign, and especially if such a sign is on the Ascendant or contains the ☽, there will be a large family. Few children only are born when the signs ♉, ♍, ♎, or ♒, occupy the above positions; and barrenness is indicated if the signs concerned are ♈, ♌, or ♑. Twins are often indicated by ♊ or ♐. Malefics in the 5th house or afflicting the ruler deny children if the signs involved are barren ones, but otherwise they cause difficulty and danger in rearing them. In a man's map the 5th house specially rules the first child, the 7th house the second child, and so on; while in a woman's map the 4th house rules the first child and the 6th the second one, etc. Step-children are ruled by the 11th house, and adopted children by the 7th. Planets in, or the rulers of, these houses are the significators of the children concerned, whose fortunes may be judged by the nature of the aspects received.

General Example. (Fig. 7, p. 51.)

The ☽ is strong by sign but badly afflicted, and is between the 7th and 4th cusps. Venus also is weak by sign and afflicted, but its position is strong as it is rising in conjunction with the ruler of the 7th. The 7th contains ♆, which is therefore the particular significator of the wife. The afflictions to the general rulers denote much delay in marriage. In a woman's map they are strong enough to deny it, for the ☉ is badly afflicted from barren signs, and ♆, the planet of renunciation, occupies the 7th. But if the map be regarded as a man's the chances are that some kind of union will take place after great delay, though the nature and severity of the afflictions suggests an irregular one. The wife is described by ♆ in ♍ as of medium height, with grey or hazel eyes and dark hair. The ☽ first applies to ♄, and as the ☽ rules the 6th (inferiors) the wife is likely to be of low birth, and the conditions of marriage rather sordid. Some peculiarity in the union is denoted by ♆ in the 7th. Details of the marriage and wife may be obtained by noting the aspects to ♆ and the houses ruled by the aspecting planets. In regard to children, all the indications are adverse excepting only the sign position of the ☽, the chief significator as it occupies the 5th. This indicates that no more than one child could be expected, and that it would stand little chance of survival. The badly afflicted state of the ☽ is an indication that the child would most probably be illegitimate.

CHAPTER XXIV

RELATIVES

The houses ruling relatives are as follows :—

Father—4th.

Mother—10th.

Brothers and sisters—3rd.

Aunts and uncles—6th (father's side) ; 12th (mother's side).

Cousins—10th (father's side) ; 4th (mother's side).

Grandparents—1st and 7th.

Grandchildren—9th.

Relatives by marriage—9th.

The houses opposite to these rule the wife or husband of the relative in question.

Planets in these houses, or the rulers, describe the relatives, and the aspects indicate the nature of the relation between them and the native. By calling the house ruling a given relative his 1st house, and renumbering the other houses accordingly, a great deal of information may be obtained about that person's affairs. Among the planets the ☉ stands for the father ; the ☽ for the mother ; ☿, ♀, and ♂ for brothers, sisters, and cousins ; ♃ for uncles ; ♄ for aged relatives ; and ♅ for grandparents. The aspects between the rulers of the 4th and 10th houses denote the harmony existing between the parents ; and the aspects between the ruler of the 1st and the significator of any relative show the kind of feeling existing between the native and the relative in question.

General Example. (Fig. 7, p. 51.)

Jupiter ruling 10th and ☿ ruling 4th are in affliction, indicating some disharmony between the parents ; a judgment supported by the mutual affliction of the ☉ and ☽. The father is described by ☿ in ♑, and this sign, together with ♒ on the 1st, which is the 10th from the 4th, suggests that he might be in Government employment. The affliction of ☿ by ♂, ruler of the 6th from the 4th, indicates that he was subject to feverish illnesses, accidents, and blood troubles (♒). The mother was rather more in sympathy with the native, but her actions were largely controlled by the father, since ♃ is weak by sign and is in a sign ruled by ☿, the father's significator. The native would receive financial help through her, owing to the rulership of ♃ over the 2nd ; its trine to ♂, part ruler of the 2nd ; and its sextile to ♅ in the 2nd. But she would be antagonistic to the wife, owing to the square to ♆ in the 7th.

The affairs of other relatives are judged similarly. Thus an aunt on the father's side (♋, a female sign, on 6th) lost her husband suddenly by an accident to his head from machinery while abroad (☽), ruling ♋, ☍ ♄, ruling her 7th and 8th, and □ ♅, ruling machinery, in her 9th in ♈, ruling the head). This method of obtaining details concerning other people is sometimes discountenanced owing to its horary nature, and the argument that such details cannot reasonably be expected to show when they do not affect the native himself, but experiment proves the remarkable accuracy of the method, and the student is advised to study it thoroughly in relation to known facts.

CHAPTER XXV

TRAVEL

The 3rd house rules short journeys such as those for business purposes or those which can be completed in a day; while the 9th rules more extended and foreign travel. The planets in, or rulers of, these houses are to be taken as the chief significators. In a general way planets in cardinal, mutable, and watery signs, and in angles or cadent houses tend to cause travel. The aspects thrown to the significators will indicate the nature and outcome of journeys. Thus afflictions from fiery signs indicate accidents; from watery signs, danger of floods and drowning; aspects from the ruler of the 6th denote travel for reasons of health; and so on.

The 4th house represents the birthplace, and if its occupant or ruler is well aspected and strong, it is better to remain at home than to travel, especially if the 9th house is afflicted. If, however, the 9th is better than the 4th, it will be well to leave the birthplace. The direction to go for success is indicated by the signs containing the benefics, if they are favourable, but otherwise those containing the best aspected planets. The points of the compass to which the signs correspond are as follows :—

♌ E	♌ E by N	♐ E by S
♉ S by E	♍ S by W	♑ S
♊ W by S	♎ W	♒ W by N
♋ N	♏ N by E	♓ N by W

These are to be taken as pointing the direction from the birthplace.

In addition to this, each sign rules certain countries, the more important of which are as follows :—

♈—England, Denmark, parts of Germany.

♉—Ireland, Poland, Persia, Asia Minor.

♊—Wales, United States of America, Lower Egypt, Belgium.

♋—Scotland, Holland, Africa, China, New Zealand, parts of Germany.

♌—France, Italy, Rumania, parts of Australia.

♍—Turkey, Switzerland, W. Indies.

♎—Austria, Japan, Upper Egypt.

♏—Algeria, Morocco, Norway, Transvaal.

♐—Spain, Hungary, parts of Australia.

♑—India, Greece, Mexico, Persia, Afghanistan.

♒—Russia, Sweden, Abyssinia, parts of Poland.

♓—Portugal, Galicia, Normandy.

The countries ruled by any sign will be favourable to the native if that sign is occupied by a well-aspected planet in his horoscope, but unfavourable if the planet is weak or afflicted.

General Example. (Fig. 7, p. 51.)

The ruler, ☿, and the ☽ in cardinal signs indicate a certain amount of travel, but it is limited to some extent by the strong fixed positions, and fixed signs on the cusps of the 3rd and 9th. Jupiter on the 4th cusp is fairly well aspected but weak, while ♂, ruler of the 9th, is also well aspected, and in conjunction with the ruler of the 4th. Hence residence either at home or abroad is fairly equally favourable, but the latter is rather better owing to the stronger position of ♂. These two bodies are the best in the horoscope, and therefore indicate the most successful places and directions for travel and residence. The sign ♒, containing ♂, indicates a place W by N off the birthplace ; while ♊ indicates W by S, so that anywhere to the West would be beneficial. The position of ♃ in ♊ points particularly to Wales or the United States. The result of residence in these places is indicated by the aspects to ♃. The affliction from ☿ in the 12th would produce enmity, and the square from ♆ in the 7th would bring matrimonial troubles or deception and public opposition, but the aspects from ♂ and ♅ promise considerable material and financial success.

CHAPTER XXVI

SOME EXAMPLE NATIVITIES

The following nativities have been chosen more or less at random on account of their general interest, and because they exemplify several departments of life. Space does not allow of a detailed reading of each, and therefore only some of the main features are mentioned.

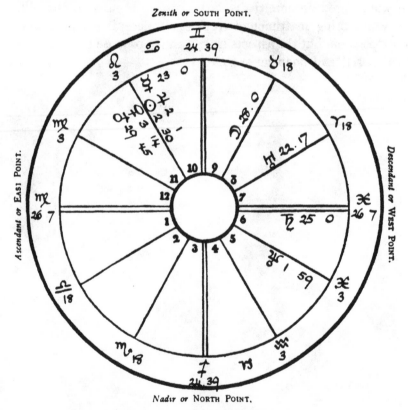

Zenith or SOUTH POINT.

Nadir or NORTH POINT.

FIG. 10.—EARL BALFOUR.

142

SOME EXAMPLE NATIVITIES

Example 1. Fig. 10.

EARL BALFOUR. Born 25th July, 1848, 9.34 a.m., Whittingehame. Died 19th March, 1930, at the age of over 81.

The ☉ is in a strong sign, and the ☽ and ascendant are in signs of moderate strength. The ☉, ruling the radical constitution, is unafflicted and in close conjunction with both the benefics ♃ and ♀, a very favourable combination. The ☽ is in its exaltation, elevated, and strongly supported by good aspects. The ascendant is also moderately strong and well aspected, except for the opposition from ♄. Note that the vital points and preserving influences all link up with each other, ☽ ✶ ☉, ☉ ✶ Ascendant, Ascendant △ ☽, thus forming a chain of strength, and with the other favourable positions, indicating a long life. Literary and philosophical work is indicated by the ☽ in the 9th house in sextile to ♄, which gives depth of thought ; and by ☿, the ruler of the 1st and 10th, elevated, also in trine to ♄. The ☉ and ♃ on the 11th cusp (Parliament) in ♌ inclined to Government work, as also did ☿ ☐ ♅, which brought public opposition at times through the square. Saturn on the 7th cusp ; ♃, ruler of 7th, and ♀ in a barren sign ; and ☽ ☐ ♆ all helped to deny marriage. By direction at death the ☉ had arrived at the opposition of the radical ♅ in the 8th house (death), and was also forming the conjunction with the progressed ♂, ruler of the 8th.

Example 2. Fig. 11.

RUPERT BROOKE. Born 3rd August, 1887, 7.32 p.m., Rugby. Died 23rd April, 1915, at the age of 27.

Here the ☉ is again in a strong sign, but both the ☽ and ascendant are weak, and ♄, the ruler, is afflicted in the 6th house. The ☉ and ☽ are in close opposition, a critical position, and the ☉ is in conjunction with ☿, ruler of the 4th. This planet is separating from the conjunction of ♄

143

and the square of ♃, and is therefore of a malefic nature. The ☽ and ascendant are badly afflicted, and all three vital points are therefore weak, and promise only a very short life.

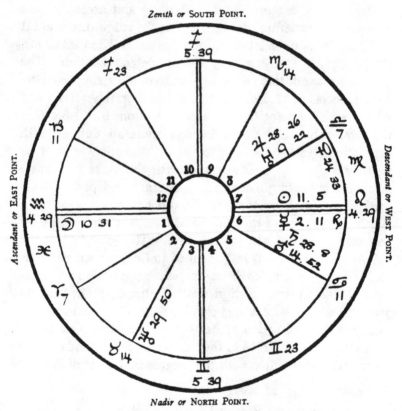

FIG. 11.—RUPERT BROOKE.

But for the radical strength by sign of the ☉ life could not have been sustained as long as it was. The horoscope is a very artistic one, with ☽ rising in ♒, ☉ and ☿ in ♌ (5th sign), ♀ angular, ♃ ruler of 10th in ♎, ♀ △ ♆, and ♅ △ ☽). Venus in ♍ inclines to poetry, as do several of the other

144

positions. Jupiter, ruler of the 10th, is in a ♀ sign, and ♀ receives the trine of ♆ in the 3rd house (writing).

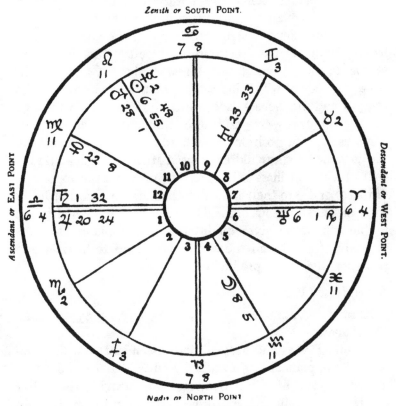

FIG. 12.—HENRY FORD.

Example 3. Fig. 12.

HENRY FORD, the millionaire motor-car manufacturer. Born 30th July, 1863, 10.0 a.m., near Detroit, Michigan, U.S.A.

The ☽, ruler of the 10th, is on the cusp of the 5th (enterprise) in ♒, a scientific sign, in trine to ♄ rising in ♎, giving

steadiness and organising ability, and in sextile to Ψ in ♈,
giving intuition. Mars, ruler of the 2nd or money house, and
one of the planets ruling the motor-car, is in the sign ♌ in
sextile to ♅, a planet of invention and organising on a large
scale, in the scientific sign ♊ in the 9th, the latter position
having brought much help from abroad. Mars is also in
sextile to the rising ♃ in the money sign ♎, and ♃ is in
trine to ♅, all of which indicate great wealth. Jupiter rules
the 3rd and 6th houses, and therefore denotes gain through
mechanical transport, and also through the goodwill of
employees. The position of the ☽, ruler of the 10th house, on
the cusp of the 5th (children) caused Mr. Ford to delegate the
control of the business to his sons for a time, but the opposition
of the ☉ and ☿ to the ☽ indicated that the step was not likely
to be an advantageous one. The position of ♅ in an airy sign
in the 9th house gives an interest in aeroplanes, but the
sesquare of the ☽ and the square of ♀ tend to hamper any
plans for their mass production.

Example 4. Fig. 13.

RUDOLPH VALENTINO. Born 6th May, 1895, 3 a.m.,
Castellaneta.

Including the mid-heaven and ascendant, the distribution of the planets is 5 Cardinal and 4 Watery, indicating
an active type of occupation, and one bringing the native
before the public. The ☉ is with ☿, ruler of the 3rd
house, in the Venusian sign ♉, attracting to artistic pursuits,
and, through the 3rd house, to work entailing movement.
Saturn, ruler of the 10th, is in the dramatic sign ♏, in trine
to ♂ and ♃ in ♋, another sign ruling acting and public
work. The ☽ is angular in the artistic sign ♎, and rules the
5th house, that of the stage. Jupiter, which is prominent
here, rules the 12th house and ♓, both of which bear rule over

the feet. Hence Valentino started his stage career as a dancer. The conjunction of ♂ with ♃ and its trine to ♄, caused him to enter a military school in his boyhood, but the fact that ♂ is in its detriment accounts for his not having

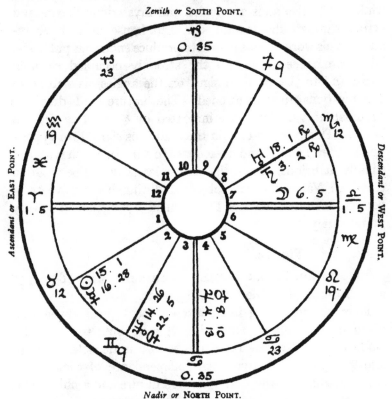

FIG. 13.—RUDOLPH VALENTINO.

adopted the Army as a career. The ☽ in the 7th house (marriage) afflicted by the squares from ♂ and ♃ in the domestic sign ♋ in the 4th (home) indicate domestic and matrimonial troubles. The amazing fascination exercised by Valentino over women is astrologically indicated by several positions.

147

The easy personal charm of the ☽ in ♎ is one factor, especially as it operates from the 7th house (the public). Then there is the intense magnetic attraction of ♏, and the trine from ♂ and ♃ in the female sign ♋, which also rules the public; while ♀☌♆ also adds an elusive and mysterious charm, and acting through the mental sign and house must have influenced his work. This helped to produce enormous publicity. His prominence is due to the strongly occupied cardinal signs, and to the cardinal signs on the angles, as well as to the positions just mentioned. The nature and dramatic circumstances of death are indicated by ♅ in ♏ in the 8th house. This position of ♅ in the malicious sign ♏, in opposition to the ☉ and ☿, and in sesquare to ♂ in ♋, which is almost equally malicious, caused the intense jealousy and persecution to which Valentino was subjected during his last years, a persecution in which the Press, ruled by ☿, played a very prominent part.

Example 5. Fig. 14.

SIR ARTHUR CONAN DOYLE. Born 22nd May, 1859, 4.55 a.m., Edinburgh. Died 7th July, 1930.

Four planets rising in ♊ altered the typical appearance given by that sign. The rising ♃ gave bulk to the body, while the effect of the ruler in ♉ is also noticeable. The ☉ and ♅ rising in ♊ give great independence of thought, to which ♂ adds quickness, and ♃ good nature and a philosophical outlook. The scientific and humanitarian sign ♒ occupies the 10th house, and its ruler is in sextile to the ☉. The strength of ♊, the literary sign, brought fame through literature. The solar conjunction with ♅ indicates quick success by originality, and is the astrological significator of Sherlock Holmes, whose characteristics are closely described by this position. The ruler, ☿, and four other planets in the

12th house also contributed to the writing of detective fiction, for this house rules mysteries and the police and detective force. Popularity was increased by the trine from the elevated ☽ in the 9th (publications) to the ☉ and ♅.

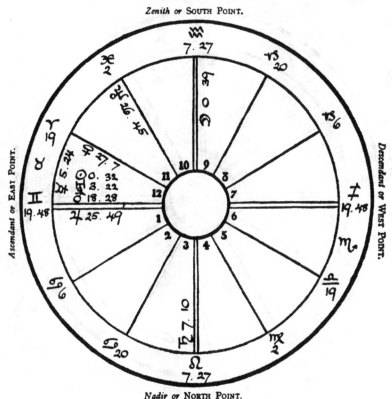

Zenith or SOUTH POINT.

Ascendant or EAST POINT.

Descendant or WEST POINT.

Nadir or NORTH POINT.

FIG. 14.—SIR A. CONAN DOYLE.

This lunar position in ♒, and the ruler in the 12th, indicate the desire to help others, and especially those considered to be unjustly imprisoned (12th). Interest in Spiritualism is indicated by the ☽ in the 9th (religion) in sextile to the psychic planet ♆, together with the strong 12th house positions. The

149

early medical work is shown by the prominence of the scientific signs, and the rising of ♃, the planet of the physician, and ♂, ruler of the 6th house (health), but its abandonment came

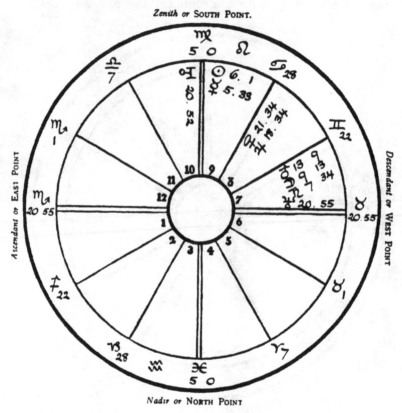

FIG. 15.—BENITO MUSSOLINI.

through the square of ♆ to ♃, and the afflicting aspects from the ☽ and ♄ to ♂. Knighthood is shown by the ☉ ☌ ♅ in sextile to ♄, ruler of the 10th (honour) in the royal sign ♌. Death by a heart affliction is very clearly shown by ♄, ruler of the 8th house (death) in ♌ (heart) on the cusp of the 4th house (end of life).

Example 6. Fig. 15.

BENITO MUSSOLINI. Born 29th July, 1883, 2 p.m. Dovia.

Power is the dominant characteristic in this chart. Five planets are angular, the strong sign ♏ is rising, and ♅, the planet of the Dictator, dominates the map from the midheaven. The ☉ is in the royal sign ♌, and ☿ in close conjunction takes on the solar nature and inclines the mind to power and rulership. The position of the ☽ in the human sign ♊, badly afflicted by being " besieged " by (i.e., in between) the malefics ♂ and ♄, is the cause of the many attempts which have been made upon the Duce's life, and which have proved unsuccessful owing to the sextile from the ☉, and also to the trine from ♀ and ♃ to the ascendant, which has great power to protect. The ruler, ♂, in ♊, the sign of the mind, in conjunction with the ☽ and ♄, the latter being ruler of the corresponding 3rd house, gives a very aggressively militant bias to the mind, and as ♊ is the sign of speech, and the planets are angular, this mental attitude is greatly to the fore in speech and writing.

Example 7. Fig. 16.

PRESIDENT HOOVER. Born 10th August, 1874, 11.15 p.m., West Branch, Iowa, U.S.A.

This is an example of the prominence given by angular planets and ♄ in the 10th. Five planets in ♌, and the ☉ in conjunction with ♅, have brought great power. President Hoover's father was a blacksmith, indicated here by ♂, the planet of fire and metals, in the 4th (father) in opposition to ♄, which when afflicting the significator of employment causes hard and dirty work. This position, together with the afflictions from ♅, also caused the father's death when the native was only nine years of age. The same position of ♄ and ♂ caused mining engineering to be chosen as a profession, but again the afflictions interfered, and finally the conjunction of the ☉ and ♅, together with the Government sign ♒ on the 10th, brought politics into the life. Saturn is strong by sign and angular, and has therefore played a part in raising Mr.

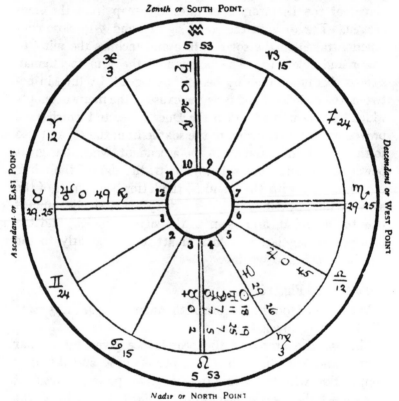

FIG. 16.—PRESIDENT HOOVER.

Hoover to the position he now occupies, but ♄ in the 10th is always a dangerous influence, and in this particular case the danger is aggravated by the opposition of the malefics in the 4th, all of which denote a sudden and serious reversal and downfall, and a dramatic political finish.

PART IV

HOW TO CALCULATE FUTURE INFLUENCES

CHAPTER XXVII

HOW TO CALCULATE DIRECTIONS

So far we have confined our attention to the horoscope of birth, and we have now to consider the subsequent changes and variations which occur in the planetary positions by which the events indicated at birth are brought to fruition. The birth horoscope is known as the Radical chart or *Radix*, for it is the root from which all changes proceed. The radical horoscope constitutes an epitome of the whole life, and nothing can ever occur that is contradictory to its indications. If the horoscope shows poverty, no subsequent influence can produce wealth. The Radix is always the primary consideration, and all changes and modifications of influence are subsidiary to those in the birth map.

The radical horoscope shows the position of the planets and signs at a definite moment, that of birth, and these are imprinted on the native throughout life. But obviously the planets in the heavens do not stop still. They continue their movements, forming fresh configurations with each other, entering other signs, and what is even more important, throwing aspects to their positions at the moment of birth. Suppose the Sun at birth is in ♈ 6. The characteristics given by this position of the Sun in ♈ will persist throughout life. But actually the Sun continues to advance after birth, and in about two months it will have reached ♊ 6. Here it will be in sextile to its own position at birth, and during those two months it will have received many aspects from other planets, and also have thrown many aspects to the places of the other planets at birth.

This movement of the planets away from their birth

155

positions bears an important relation to the life of the native, for upon it depends the age at which events occur, and also the particular nature of the events. It has been found that a movement of one degree is equivalent to one year of life, and also that planetary changes taking place in one day are equivalent to one year. These two measures of time as they are called, which are actually very closely related, form the basis of the two chief systems of predictive astrology. In the system called Primary, we measure the number of degrees of Right Ascension which pass over the midheaven while a planet passes to the conjunction or aspect of another, taking one as moving and the other as fixed, and turn these degrees into time at the rate of one degree for a year. The result is the age of the native at which the effect of the aspect will be felt. In actual practice the process of calculation is complicated and tedious, and the system falls quite outside the scope of the present work.

In the Secondary system, which is that in common use, we are concerned with the motion of the planets on the days following birth, each day after birth representing one year of life. The movement of the planets day by day away from their birth positions is known as *Progression*, and the aspects formed either among themselves or to the planets in the birth horoscope are called *Directions*. The calculation of Secondary Directions is quite simple. The planetary positions at birth not only represent the whole life, but in a more particular sense they show the events of the first year of life. The positions on the day after birth show the events occurring between the first anniversary of the birthday and the second. The positions on the thirtieth day after birth indicate the events of the thirtieth year of life, and so on.

In its simplest form the process consists in erecting a horoscope for the same time as birth on each day after birth. In our example horoscope (Fig. 7) birth took place at 7.33 a.m.

on 10th February, 1930, at Liverpool. The horoscope as it stands represents in a special way the events of life during the first year, namely from 10th February, 1930, to 9th February, 1931. If we erect another horoscope for 7.33 a.m., on 11th February, 1930, we obtain the progressed positions for the first birthday on 10th February, 1931, and this map shows the events occurring between 10th February, 1931, and 9th February, 1932. If we wish to know what will happen when the native is 25 years old, we simply count 25 days after birth, which brings us to 7th March, 1930, and erect a map for 7.33 a.m. on that day. The positions so obtained are the progressed places for the 25th year after birth, namely 10th February, 1955 to 9th February, 1956. The aspects formed between the planets themselves, and their aspects to the radical positions on the day in question are worked out, and the exact date in the year to which they correspond is easily found by proportion.

As an example we will calculate the directions formed in the horoscope of King George V during 1928-1929, measuring to the period of his serious illness.

King George was born at Marlborough House (37 secs. West Long.) on 3rd June, 1865, at 1h 20m 6s a.m., the horoscope being as in Fig. 17.

On 3rd June, 1928, the King attained the age of 63 years, and therefore we must erect the progressed horoscope for 63 days after birth. Count the days carefully, calling the actual day of birth o. Thus :—

3rd June 1865 is age 0
4th   ,,   ,,   ,,   1
5th   ,,   ,,   ,,   2
6th   ,,   ,,   ,,   3

and so on.

Continuing, we find that age 63 corresponds to 5th August,

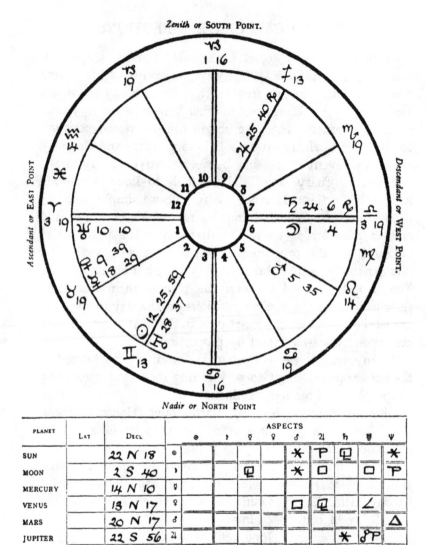

FIG. 17.—KING GEORGE V.

158

1865. Therefore if we erect a horoscope for 1.20 a.m. on 5th August, 1865 it will give us the progressed positions for 3rd June, 1928, and the movement and aspects of the

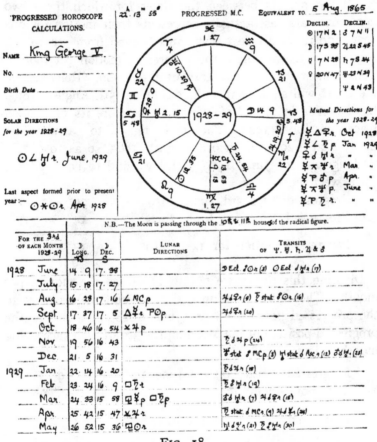

FIG. 18.

planets between 1.20 a.m. on 5th August, 1865, and 1.20 a.m. on 6th August, 1865 will represent the events occurring between June 1928 and June 1929.

The progressed horoscope is shown in Fig. 18.

This horoscope shows the progressed positions for 3rd June, 1928, and a horoscope for exactly twenty-four hours later shows them for 3rd June, 1929. Therefore the daily motion of all the planets between the times for which these two horoscopes are cast actually represents their motion for one year, and if we divide the distance moved from 5th to 6th August by 12 we obtain the progressed motion per month. This is most rapid in the case of the Moon. Reference to the chart will show that at 1.20 a.m. on 5th August, 1865, the Moon is in ♑ 14° 9', which is therefore its progressed place for June, 1928. The next step is to calculate its position at 1.20 a.m. on 6th August, 1865, so as to obtain its longitude for June, 1929. This we find to be ♑ 28° 1'. Then we have :—

Progressed ☽ for 3rd June, 1929	..	28° 1' ♑
Progressed ☽ for 3rd June, 1928	..	14° 9 ♑
Progressed motion for 12 months	..	13° 52'

Dividing this by 12 we obtain 1° 9⅓' as the motion per month. Therefore by adding this amount successively to the progressed position on 3rd June, 1928, we arrive at the progressed position of the Moon on the 3rd of each succeeding month. Thus:

Progressed position on 3rd June, 1928 ..	14° 9'	♑
Add monthly motion	1 9⅓	
Progressed position on 3rd July, 1928 ..	15 18⅓	♑
Add monthly motion	1 9⅓	
Progressed position on 3rd August, 1928	16 27⅔	♑

Continue in this way and then tabulate the results correct to the nearest minute as shown in Fig. 18.

The same process should be performed with the Moon's progressed declination.

Now take each planet in the radical horoscope and see whether the progressed Moon makes any aspect to it during the twelve months. If so, enter the aspect against the appropriate month and put a little " r " after the planet to indicate that the aspect is thrown to its radical position.

The radical ☉ in King George's horoscope is in ♊ 12° 26'. The sesquare to this falls in ♑ 27° 26', and the progressed ☽ reaches this point during May, 1929. It forms no aspect to its own place during the year. The radical ☿ is in ♉ 18° 29', and the ☽ forms the trine to this when it reaches ♑ 18° 29'. Reference to the tabulated positions shows that the ☽ is in this point during September, 1928, so we enter ☽△ ☿ r. against that month. Continue in this way until each radical planet has been examined, and then do the same over again with the declinations of the radical planets using the Moon's progressed declination, and note any parallels against the month in which they are exactly formed.

Now turn to the progressed map and see in which months the Moon aspects the progressed places of the planets. Note these down and place a little " p " after the planet to indicate that it is the progressed position that is aspected. It may be mentioned here that the usual custom is always to write the moving body first, so there is no need to mark the first-mentioned planet as progressed. In the case of the progressed positions care is sometimes needed in ascertaining the correct month in which the aspect falls. For example, in the King's progressed chart ☿ is in ♍ 9°13'. This chart is correct for 3rd June, 1928, but between that date and 3rd June, 1929 (i.e., between 5th and 6th August, 1865), ☿ moves to ♍ 10° 24', a distance of 1° 11', which gives a monthly motion of nearly 6'. Therefore we have to make a table of Mercury's monthly position and compare the progressed ☽ with that. By this means we see that the lunar sesquare to ☿ p. is really formed in March, and not in February as would appear if we used the position for June as it is in the progressed chart.

Having worked out all the aspects to progressed planets repeat the process with the declinations instead of the longitudes.

Finally, if the birth horoscope is correct in regard to time, note the aspects formed by the progressed ☽ to the radical and progressed Ascendant and Midheaven. If, however, the time is uncertain it is of little use to calculate directions to angles. The midheaven progresses at the rate of about 1° a year, and in the radical chart this represents a period of about 4 minutes, so that an error of 4 minutes in the birth-time will throw these directions out by about a year. This does not apply to directions between the Sun, Moon, and planets, which are not greatly affected by a quite considerable error in the birth-time.

We have now calculated all the lunar directions, and it remains to work out those formed by the other bodies. These are sometimes termed primary directions because they are of greater power than the lunar ones, but the term is mis-leading since it properly refers to another system altogether, and it is better to call these directions *Basic*, and divide them into *Solar* directions, which include those formed by the progressed Sun and to the radical Sun, and *Mutual*, which include all other directions amongst the planets themselves.

First take the progressed ☉. This moves about 1° in the year, or 5′ a month, its exact motion being obtained by subtraction. At 1.20 a.m. on 5th August, 1865 (equivalent to June, 1928) the ☉ is in ♌ 12° 35′, and at 1.20 a.m. on 6th August, 1865 (equivalent to June, 1929) it is in ♌ 13° 33′. This gives a progressed motion of 58′ for the year, or just under 5' a month. See whether it forms any aspect during this period to any of the radical planets. The radical ♅ is in ♊ 28° 37' and the progressed ☉ will be in semisquare to it when it reaches ♌ 13° 37'. This will be exact at the end of June, 1929, and is really outside the period, but in the case of the major directions it is necessary to examine the influences in operation both before and after the required period for a reason which will appear when we come to the rules of interpretation.

This is the only aspect formed by the progressed ☉ to the radical planets. Next note whether any parallels are formed by the ☉ by comparing its progressed declination with that of each of the radical bodies. In this case there are none.

Now see whether the progressed ☉ forms any aspects and parallels to the progressed planets, excepting the progressed ☽ which has already been examined.

Having completed the aspects formed by the progressed ☉, take each progressed planet in turn, beginning with ☿, and note any aspects and parallels it may form to the radical and progressed places of all the other bodies. Note them down with the month in which they are exact.

Finally, if the time is accurate, note any aspects formed by the progressed ascendant and midheaven to the radical and progressed planets, and also any aspects formed by the progressed planets to the radical ascendant and midheaven.

You have now a complete survey of all the Secondary directions in operation during the required period, as shown in Fig. 18.

The process may be summarised as follows :—

1. Prog. Moon to aspects and parallels of radical planets and angles.

2. Prog. Moon to aspects and pars. of prog. planets and angles.

3. Prog. Sun to aspects and pars. of radical planets and angles.

4. Prog. Sun to aspects and pars. of prog. planets and angles.

5. Prog. planets to aspects and pars. of radical planets and angles.

6. Prog. planets to aspects and pars. of prog. planets and angles.

7. Prog. angles to aspects of radical planets.

8. Prog. angles to aspects of prog. planets.

This takes some little time to complete, but it should be done conscientiously and not skipped, for it is easy to overlook an important direction which may modify the whole interpretation.

TRANSITS

When all the directions have been ascertained there is still a final step left, and that is to note the important transits. Transits are the passages of the planets day by day in the current ephemeris over the places and aspects of the planets in the radical and progressed charts. It is important not to confuse motion by transit with motion by progression. To find the transits it is necessary to use an ephemeris for the actual year for which the directions are required. In our example the progressed positions for 1928 are those shown in the 1865 ephemeris for 5th August. But to find the transits for 1928 we require an ephemeris for the actual year 1928 itself, from which we can see when the planets during 1928 pass over or aspect the planets in the radical and progressed charts. Thus on 8th August 1928 ♃ passes over the place of ♀ in the King's birth horoscope ; on 24th November ♄ passes over the progressed place of ♃, and so on.   It is usual to note only the conjunctions and oppositions of Mars, Jupiter, Saturn, Uranus, and Neptune by transit.   The transits of the Moon, Mercury, and Venus are too quick to be of great importance, and usually indicate little more than good or bad days.   Raphael has published a shilling booklet giving the positions of the major planets on the first of each month from 1900 to 2001 which will be found of use in the case of future years where no ephemeris is available.

The transit effect of planets by square and trine is also appreciable, but to use all such aspects tends rather to confusion by multiplying the factors to be taken into consideration.

The position of eclipses and new Moons are also to be regarded as transits, the former being of very great importance.

This completes the survey of the influences at work during any particular year by the Secondary system of directing. It may be mentioned here that there is a method, known as the Noon Date method, by means of which some of the calculation may be simplified. This method, however, though quite easy in itself, is usually found somewhat confusing by the beginner, and I have therefore thought it better to omit all particulars of it and let the student come to it later in his studies after he is familiar with the general process.

CHAPTER XXVIII

HOW TO JUDGE DIRECTIONS

Having worked out the directions in operation for any required period it is necessary to interpret them, and the rules for this are the same for any system of directing.

1. First of all it is essential to have made a study of the birth horoscope, and to bear that in mind throughout. As already mentioned, the radical chart covers the whole life, and if it shows poverty no direction however good can bring riches. If the birth map indicates difficulty and delay in marriage, it is useless to expect a direction to Venus in the twenties to mark more than a passing attachment. The radical nature and strength of the planets indicates their power in directions. If Jupiter is badly afflicted at birth it will produce little good by direction even under strongly benefic aspects. Any planet afflicted at birth will operate with greater strength under bad directions than under good ones, and conversely, any planet, even a malefic, that is well aspected at birth will bring benefit under good directions ; and its harmful effect under evil ones will be considerably mitigated. Failure to take this into account is the cause of frequent error in prediction.

2. Pay greatest attention to the aspects of the Sun, planets, and angles, rather than to those of the Moon, for the former remain in force for a period of several months and indicate the general tone and nature of the period. The directions of each planet form a chain, and a direction formed by any planet should be considered in the light of the last one it formed and the next. If a good direction is sandwiched in between bad ones its effect is greatly minimised, while a bad direction

166

in a chain of good ones does little harm. In the case of the chain of directions formed by a single planet, a critical point is formed midway between directions of an opposite nature. Thus suppose the ☉ were in square to ♄ in June, 1930, and next formed the sextile to ♃ in October, 1934. The midpoint between these dates is August 1932, and that would be the turning point from the bad influence to the good one.

3. In estimating the effect of a direction we have to consider the general effect of the planets in aspect, the signs and houses in which they are placed, and the houses they rule. Chief consideration is to be paid to the radical house positions and the radical houses ruled, especially in the case of a progressed body aspecting a radical one. Here we consider the house and sign containing the radical planet, and the house and sign in the radical chart into which the progressed body has moved. In the case of two progressed bodies the influence of the houses in the progressed chart is sometimes appreciable, but the student will find it safest to disregard the progressed map, and base his interpretations entirely upon the radical houses.

Suppose, for example, that the ☉ had passed to the sextile of the place of ♃ at birth, or in other words, that the direction ☉ ✶ ♃ r. were formed. By its own nature the aspect is expansive, and tends to good luck, financial benefit, business advancement, etc. If ♃ were in the 2nd house at birth we should expect money matters to be chiefly concerned, and if it were also in ♏ the benefit might come through a death. If it ruled the 9th house the benefit might come from abroad, or possibly from one of the wife's relatives ; if the 10th, there would be business advancement and monetary benefit through the death of a superior, and so on. Then the position of the ☉ would still further refine the judgment through the house and sign it had passed into, and also its radical signification.

167

As a general rule the moving planet imports its influence to the things signified by the radical planet. Thus it is possible by a careful study of the strength of the planets and the houses and signs involved to obtain an intimate knowledge of the exact effects likely to be produced by the aspect in any given horoscope. In the next chapter will be found an account of the general effect of directions, but it will be obvious from the above remarks that everything depends upon the particular conditions of the horoscope, and that no book can possibly contain the effects of every combination and variation of house and sign. The most that can be done is to give a general idea of the kind of effect that follows a direction between any two planets, and leave the student to fill in the details himself.

4. The lunar directions are of far less importance than the Basic ones, and too much stress should not be laid upon them. This is a frequent error made by the beginner, who is apt to predict dire misfortune simply on the strength of, say, a lunar square to Saturn. The function of the lunar aspects is to point out the time when the major directions will work, and also to mark the unimportant, or at least less important, monthly influences. The action of the lunar directions depends very largely upon the Basic ones in force at the time. The Basic directions give the general nature and colouring, and if they are adverse then the good lunar directions will be largely suppressed and the bad ones act with greater intensity. Conversely, if the Basic directions are good, then good lunar ones act strongly, and bad ones are ineffective. If the period is a transition one between good and bad Basic directions, then the lunar ones act strongly according to their own nature. The Basic directions tend to act close to the month in which they are exactly formed, but their operation may be hastened or retarded by lunar directions. The Moon

acts as a focusing influence, and when it aspects a planet that is also one of the bodies forming a Basic direction the latter will be stimulated to action even if not quite exact. Similarly a Basic direction may be revived after it has begun to pass off in the same way.   In this way, a good lunar direction may stimulate a bad Basic one, or vice versa.   Thus with ☉ ⚹ ♃ r. in force, any aspect to either of these bodies will excite the direction.   If ☽ □ ☉ or ☽ □ ♃, for example, be formed at about this time, the major effect will be evoked. In this case the effect would begin with some slightly adverse circumstances owing to the lunar square, but would improve rapidly.   In the case of a major square or opposition excited by a lunar trine or sextile, the effect would seem favourable at first but would rapidly become evil.   If the lunar direction is of the same nature as the Basic, then the matter would start well or badly according to the nature of both directions. Acting alone, however, the lunar directions follow the nature of the aspect in the ordinary way.

Transits fulfil the same function as lunar directions in this respect, and the transit of a major planet will stimulate a direction if it passes over, or strongly aspects, the radical or progressed place of either body involved.   In this case the radical sign and house position of the transiting body as well as its own nature will be involved in the effect.   Thus Mars by transit will excite a direction through haste, headstrong action, fire, wounds, illness, etc., the exact cause and nature being indicated by its position in the birth horoscope.

5.   Eclipses falling in conjunction or opposition to any important planet are evil in their effect.   They usually signify misfortune, death, or the cutting off of the matters or people signified by the planet upon, or opposite, which they fall. Their effect lasts about four years as a rule, and is stimulated from time to time by transits over the eclipse point.

Important eclipses coinciding with a train of bad directions are of the greatest significance and danger.

6. Directions are cumulative in effect. A single direction of any nature does not usually produce an effect of the first magnitude, and the greatest results come from a series or chain of directions of the same nature, either good or bad. A series of bad aspects gradually reduces the native in health or affairs, each aspect adding a little to the work of its predecessor. Frequently it will be found that a long train of evil directions ends abruptly, and after a blank the aspects are good or mixed. This usually means that the effect of the evil chain works up to a climax with its last direction and smashes up the conditions so that the native is forced to begin again or to encounter entirely different conditions of life.

Now let us examine the King's directions which we calculated in the last chapter. The ☉ is passing from the sextile of its own place to the semisquare of ♅. The mid-point is formed in November 1928, and from that date the adverse aspect may be considered to begin. The radical ♅ is in ♊ in the 3rd house, and the progressed ☉ is in ♌ on the cusp of the radical 6th. Here we have a direction which produces sudden disasters. The ☉ is operating from the 6th house indicating that the health is in danger of sudden and unexpected attack. The position of ♅ in the sign ♊ clearly indicates the lungs as one of the principal points of danger, the other being the heart, as shown by the solar position in ♌. The cause of the illness appears to be a short journey, owing to the 3rd house and ♊ afflictions. As ♄ had been transiting the opposition of the ☉ and was within orbs of the opposition of ♅ in November, we should expect the immediate cause of the illness to be a chill, ruled by ♄, taken on a short journey in connection with public affairs, the latter being indicated by the radical position of ♄ in the 7th house. The illness did not come earlier under the exact transit of ♄ over the opposition of the ☉ because at the time that was formed the Basic and lunar directions were all favourable, and remained so until the end of October, preventing serious trouble until after that date.

The Mutual directions intensified the Solar, being of a similar nature. The semisquare of ☿ to ♄ began to operate in November, and also affected the lungs and health through Mercury's rulership over ♊, and also ♍, which occupies the 6th house. The next Mutual direction was the conjunction of Venus and Uranus in January. This brought Venus to the place of Uranus, and improved the evil conditions, marking the turning-point towards recovery. No lunar directions measured to the worst period of the illness, but the transits were serious. The announcement was made on the 21st November, and the 24th and 25th were critical days owing to the transit of ♄ over ♃. In December, on the day when ♅ was exactly stationary on the radical ascendant, the operation for drainage was performed ; and in January the bulletins became definitely reassuring. In April, under ☽ ⚹ ♃ r., the period of danger had passed, and the King was well on the road to recovery.

CHAPTER XXIX

The following descriptions briefly summarise the general effects of directions according to the natures of the planets forming them. These should be modified and amplified by a consideration of the signs and houses involved in the particular horoscope, as explained in the preceding chapter.

I. DIRECTIONS OF THE ANGLES

Asc.—☉

♂ or Good. Honour; good health; gain through Government or influential people. Sometimes marriage or childbirth in a woman's map.

Bad. Bad health; enmity of influential people; loss of employment; danger to the father.

Asc.—☽

♂ or Good. Journeys; changes; voyages; public success; popularity; attachments; marriage or childbirth.

Bad. Illness; unpopularity; unfortunate changes and journeys; matrimonial troubles and discord.

Asc.—☿

♂ or Good. Travel; mental and bodily activity; change of residence; gain by writing or teaching.

Bad. Worry; nervous disorders; liable to fraud or slander; failure at school or college, or in literary work.

Asc.—♀

♂ or Good. Pleasure; financial gain; success in artistic work; purchase of furniture or luxuries; attachment or marriage; birth of a child.

Bad. Heavy expenses; extravagance; trouble through women and attachments; danger to female relatives; intemperance; illness.

Asc.—♂

Good. Travel; martial exercises or occupation; great activity, attachments; childbirth. Sometimes marriage in a woman's map.

♂ or Bad. Feverish and inflammatory diseases, accidents, and operations; danger to a parent; loss by quarrels and disputes, and disfavour of others.

Asc.— ♃

♂ or Good. Social success; new friends; advancement; financial success; favours from nobility; birth of child.

Bad. Illness, blood and liver disorders; intemperate; loss through false friends or extravagance, and by the law; failure of hopes.

Asc.—♄

Good. Inheritance; gain by property, may receive legacy; benefit through elderly people.

♂ or Bad. Accidents; colds, chills, rheumatism, or lingering illnesses; loss and disappointments; trouble through elderly people, houses, and property.

Asc.—♅

Good. Unexpected benefits; fortunate journeys; gain through public concerns; romantic attachments.

♂ or Bad. Sudden illness; nervous disorders, accidents, or operation; sudden losses; danger to a parent.

Asc.—♆

Good. Pleasant travel; voyages; financial gain; peculiar experiences; musical or psychic interests.

Bad. Nervous disorders; loss by travel and by fraud; confinement in hospital or institution.

173

M.C.—☉

♂ *or Good.* Honour, advancement ; renown ; gain by public office. Sometimes marriage in a woman's map.

Bad. Loss of employment ; disgrace ; bankruptcy ; loss by superiors ; loss of a parent or husband.

M.C.—☽

♂ *or Good.* Voyage or complete change ; favourable business changes ; benefit from women or the public ; marriage or birth of child.

Bad. Unpopularity ; scandal ; loss through women or the public ; domestic troubles ; danger to wife or mother.

M.C.—☿

♂ *or Good.* New enterprises ; travel ; change of residence ; gain by teaching, writing, or the law.

Bad. Loss by writing, correspondence, law, and travel ; danger of libel and false accusations ; death of a child or relative.

M.C.—♀

♂ or *Good.* Pleasure ; prosperity ; free expenditure ; artistic pursuits ; attachment or marriage ; birth of child.

Bad. Extravagance ; dissipation ; scandal ; loss through women and by jealousy or rashness ; trouble to female relatives.

M.C.—♂

Good. Enterprising ; active time ; journeys, success in martial occupations.

♂ *or Bad.* Heavy losses ; quarrels ; illness, accident, or operation ; loss by fire or theft ; death of a parent.

M.C.— ♃

♂ *or Good.* Success and honour ; great gain and prosperity. Often causes marriage in a woman's map.

Bad. Heavy expenses ; financial disputes ; loss in business or by law ; social difficulties.

M.C.—♄

Good. Responsibility or position of trust ; general advancement ; inheritance ; gain through elderly people or superiors.

♂ or Bad. Loss of reputation and credit ; dishonour ; loss of employment ; unpopularity ; death of a parent.

M.C.—♅

Good. Sudden and unexpected gain or advancement ; sudden changes ; travel ; gain by invention or public concerns.

♂ or Bad. Discredit ; sudden family and business troubles ; political losses ; death of a parent or grandparent.

M.C.—♆

Good. Gain ; good business ; gain by travel ; idealistic attachments ; musical or psychic interests.

Bad. Loss by travel and fraud ; business losses and disappointments ; danger of discredit and of peculiar slander ; danger to a parent.

II. SOLAR DIRECTIONS

☉—☽

Good. Business and financial success ; advancement ; new enterprises ; change of residence ; marriage.

Bad. Loss of money ; unemployment ; illness or eye trouble ; adverse changes ; bereavement or death of relative.

The ♂ is critical, and depends upon the radical aspects of the ☉ and ☽, and the other directions in operation. To a woman it often brings illness, and to a man, marriage.

☉—☿

♂ or Good. Busy period ; literary activity ; travel ; many changes ; birth of child.

175

Bad. Danger of fraud ; false accusations ; illness ; trouble through writing, documents and the law.

$$\odot - ♀$$

☌ *or Good.* Pleasure ; happy and prosperous period ; artistic interests ; attachment or marriage.

Bad. Loss ; extravagance ; dissipation ; disappointment in love ; trouble through women.

$$\odot - ♂$$

Good. Physical activity ; good health and vitality ; distinction in martial occupations. May bring marriage in a woman's map.

☌ *or Bad.* Fevers ; accidents ; wounds ; quarrels ; loss by fire, disputes, and lawsuits ; danger to a parent.

$$\odot - ♃$$

☌ *or Good.* Good health ; general prosperity ; honour and wealth ; new and powerful friends. Often brings marriage in a woman's map.

Bad. Financial loss ; business troubles ; great opposition ; loss by law ; blood and liver disorders.

$$\odot - ♄$$

Good. Gain from buildings and property ; public reputation ; advancement ; gain through elderly people and by legacy.

☌ *or Bad.* Misfortunes ; loss of money and position ; grief and sorrow ; bereavement ; danger of lowered vitality, heart weakness, and accidents.

$$\odot - ♅$$

Good. Travel ; beneficial changes ; gain by invention ; public or municipal advancement. Hasty attachment or marriage in a woman's map.

☌ *or Bad.* Sudden calamities ; loss of position ; danger of accident or neurasthenia. Domestic separation or liaisons, especially in a woman's map.

⊙—♆

Good. Travel; business benefit; psychic experiences; musical interests.

♂ or Bad. Disappointments; danger of fraud; crisis in affairs; confinement in hospital or institution.

III. MUTUAL DIRECTIONS

☿—♀

Good. Pleasant period; artistic interests; social success; new friends.

Bad. Heavy expenditure or extravagance; trouble through women; loss by artistic pursuits.

☿—♂

Good. Mental and physical activity; business increase; success in martial pursuits and study.

Bad. Quarrels; loss by theft or fraud; danger of libel; loss by law.

☿—♃

Good. Popularity; business advancement; gain by writing, speculation, or the law.

Bad. Danger from libel, forgery, and perjury; legal losses; loss by speculation; mental derangement.

☿—♄

Good. Inclines to study, seriousness, and steady progress; business advancement and promotion.

Bad. Quarrels; danger of theft; loss through undesirable friends.

☿—♅

Good. Occult interests; travel; gain by invention or in unusual ways.

177

Bad. Trouble through writings; involved in newspaper controversies; danger of nervous breakdown.

☿—♅

Good. Travel; psychic interests; new and peculiar friendships; gain through imaginative writing.

Bad. Worry; vague fears; hypochondria; mental perversion; loss by fraud and deception.

♀—♂

Good. Free expenditure; love of pleasure and opposite sex; rather dangerous in a woman's map.

Bad. Extravagance; quarrels; flirtations; scandal; dissipation; low female company; domestic trouble.

♀—♃

Good. Success; financial benefits; social pleasures; help from women.

Bad. Squanders money on pleasure, women, or adornment; pride; loss by speculation; domestic trouble or separation.

♀—♄

Good. Financial gain by industry or investment; binding attachment.

Bad. Financial loss; grief, sorrow, and bereavement; undesirable friendships; disgrace through women.

♀—♅

Good. Social pleasures; flirtations or liaisons; romantic love affairs; sudden financial gain.

Bad. Scandal; broken attachments, separation, and divorce; illicit love affairs.

♀—♆

Good. Peculiar friendships; pleasant holiday; artistic or poetical success; idealistic attachments.

Bad. Financial loss by fraud; undesirable attachments or pleasures; deception in love or marriage.

178

♂— ♃

Good. Energy; promotion; honour and success; gain by speculation.

Bad. Extravagance; loss by hastiness or recklessness, and by lawsuits and speculation.

♂—♄

Good. Courageous and energetic; some distinction; increased authority and responsibility.

Bad. Irritability and anger; many quarrels; malice; violence; liable to serious accidents, or to illness or operations.

♂—♅

Good. Success in litigation or against opposition; gain through inventions, engineering, and through quick action.

Bad. Business and domestic trouble; quarrels; danger of explosions and accidents; sudden illness.

♂—♆

Good. Travel; increase of pleasure; religious enthusiasm; success in hazardous enterprises.

Bad. Tends to sensuality; perverted desires; emotional or physical violence; trouble through hasty impulses.

Any progressed aspects which may be formed between ♃, ♄, ♅, and ♆ will usually be within orbs at birth, and will produce an effect similar to that indicated by the birth aspect. The description of these will be found in Chapter XIV.

IV. LUNAR DIRECTIONS

☽—☉

Good. Gain; business increase; new ventures; financial success; new friends; marriage.

Bad. General misfortune; illness; loss of money or business; bereavement.

179

♂ Bad for women, indicating changes in the system. With men it acts like the good aspects, but may adversely affect the eyes or health.

☽—☽

♂ or *Good.* The ☽ in favourable aspect to its own place at birth brings changes, holidays, journeys, removal of residence, gain by women, and new friendships.

Bad. Loss; disappointment; unpopularity; trouble through women and the public; adverse changes or removals.

☽—☿

♂ or *Good.* Business activity; changes; journeys; literary work; success in study; gain through legal affairs or people.

Bad. Small worries and annoyances; restless mind; nerve troubles; adverse criticism and slander; loss by writing, agreements, and the law; failure in examinations and study.

☽—♀

♂ or *Good.* Pleasure; happiness; social success; courtship or marriage; birth of child; good fortune.

Bad. Extravagance; irregular habits; scandal; disappointment in love; illness; domestic troubles; bereavement; loss or trouble through women.

☽—♂

Good. Busy and active time; new enterprises; journeys; physical exercise and sport; gain through martial people or things; in woman's map, impulsive attachments.

♂ or *Bad.* Danger of fevers, accidents, and loss of blood; impulsive action; extravagance; discredit and slander; quarrels and disputes; undesirable friends; trouble through opposite sex.

☽— ♃

☌ *or Good.* Prosperity; financial success; promotion; achievement of ambitions; free expenditure; beneficial attachments and friendships; good health.

Bad. Extravagance; many expenses; business losses; loss by speculation; imposed upon by friends; loss by law or professional people; blood or liver disorders.

☽—♄

Good. Steady business success; industry and patience; gain by legacy, and through elderly people; advancement; responsible position.

☌ *or Bad.* Business and financial loss and failure; disappointment; sorrow and depression; bereavement; narrow and suspicious mental outlook; slander and dishonour; illness through colds, chills, etc.

☽—♅

Good. Sudden journeys or changes; unexpected benefits; romantic attachments; occult interests.

☌ *or Bad.* Unexpected losses and troubles; accidents; loss through public bodies; unfortunate changes; disgrace or loss of employment; danger in travel; illicit love affairs.

☽—♆

Good. Pleasant journey or holiday by water or at the seaside; gain through speculation; artistic success; musical and psychic interests.

Bad. Loss by fraud, deception, or plots; vague fears and worries; disappointments; hospital experiences; depleted vitality; chaotic or perverted desires.

INDEX

INDEX

INDEX

Better books make better astrologers.
Here are some of our other titles:

AstroAmerica's Daily Ephemeris, 2010-2020
AstroAmerica's Daily Ephemeris, 2000-2020
   - both for Midnight. Compiled & formatted by David R. Roell

Al Biruni
The Book of Instructions in the Elements of the Art of Astrology,
   1029 AD, translated by R. Ramsay Wright

Derek Appleby
Horary Astrology: The Art of Astrological Divination

E. H. Bailey
The Prenatal Epoch

Joseph Blagrave
Astrological Practice of Physick

C.E.O. Carter
The Astrology of Accidents
An Encyclopaedia of Psychological Astrology
Essays on the Foundations of Astrology
The Principles of Astrology, *Intermediate no. 1*
Some Principles of Horoscopic Delineation, *Intermediate no. 2*
Symbolic Directions in Modern Astrology
The Zodiac and the Soul

Charubel & Sepharial
Degrees of the Zodiac Symbolized, *1898*

Nicholas Culpeper
Astrological Judgement of Diseases from the Decumbiture of the
   Sick, *1655, and,* **Urinalia,** *1658*

Dorotheus of Sidon
Carmen Astrologicum, *c. 50 AD, translated by David Pingree*

Nicholas deVore
Encyclopedia of Astrology

Firmicus Maternus
Ancient Astrology Theory & Practice: Matheseos Libri VIII,
c. 350 AD, translated by Jean Rhys Bram

William Lilly
Christian Astrology, books 1 & 2, *1647*
   The Introduction to Astrology, Resolution of all manner of questions.
Christian Astrology, book 3, *1647*
   Easie and plaine method teaching how to judge upon nativities.

Alan Leo
The Progressed Horoscope, *1905*

Jean-Baptiste Morin
The Cabal of the Twelve Houses Astrological, *translated by George Wharton, edited by D.R. Roell*

Claudius Ptolemy
Tetrabiblos, *c. 140 AD, translated by J.M. Ashmand*
The great book, in the classic translation.

Vivian Robson
Astrology and Sex
Electional Astrology
Fixed Stars & Constellations in Astrology
A Student's Text-Book of Astrology

Diana Roche
The Sabian Symbols, A Screen of Prophecy

Richard Saunders
The Astrological Judgement and Practice of Physick, *1677*
By the Richard who inspired Ben Franklin's famous Almanac.

Sepharial
Primary Directions, a definitive study
A complete, detailed guide.

Sepharial On Money. *For the first time in one volume, complete texts:*

- **Law of Values**
- **Silver Key**
- **Arcana, or Stock and Share Key** — *first time in print!*

James Wilson, Esq.
Dictionary of Astrology
From 1820. Quirky, opinionated, a fascinating read.

H.S. Green, Raphael & C.E.O. Carter
Mundane Astrology: *3 Books, complete in one volume.*
A comprehensive guide to political astrology

If not available from your local bookseller, order directly from:
The Astrology Center of America
207 Victory Lane
Bel Air, MD 21014

on the web at:
http://www.astroamerica.com